OFFICE XP PROFESSIONAL

STEPHEN COPESTAKE

BARNES
&NOBLE
BOOKS
NEW YORK

In easy steps is an imprint of Computer Step
Southfield Road . Southam
Warwickshire CV47 0FB . United Kingdom
www.ineasysteps.com

This edition published for Barnes & Noble Books, New York
FOR SALE IN THE USA ONLY
www.bn.com

Notice of Liability
Every effort has been made to ensure that this book contains
accurate and current information. However, Computer Step and the
author shall not be liable for any loss or damage suffered by readers
as a result of any information contained herein.

Trademarks
Microsoft®, Windows® and Office XP® are registered trademarks of
Microsoft Corporation. All other trademarks are acknowledged as
belonging to their respective companies.

Printed and bound in the United Kingdom

ISBN 0-7607-4783-0

Contents

Excel 2002   95

3

Outlook 2002   141

4

PowerPoint 2002   157

5

6 **Access 2002** **185**

7 **Mail merging** **225**

Index **23**

A common approach

This chapter shows you how to get started quickly in any Office XP module. You'll create new documents and open/save existing ones. You'll use the Shortcut bar to save time and effort, and also ask questions and get answers via Ask-a-Question.

Finally, you'll edit files from Internet Explorer and enhance your use of Office with additional features (these include Quick File Switching, error repair, copying/pasting multiple items, using the Task Pane and signing documents digitally).

Covers

Introduction

Microsoft Office XP Professional consists of these modules:

- Word 2002 – word-processor

- Excel 2002 – spreadsheet

- Outlook 2002 – personal/business information manager

- PowerPoint 2002 – presentation/slide show creator

- Access 2002 – database

There are many new features in Office XP – see later in this chapter. One which is especially useful for Web use, however, is the ability to target Web output at specific browsers.

In any module apart from Access and Outlook, pull down the Tools menu and click Options. In the Options dialog, select the General tab and click Web Options. In the Web Options dialog, select the Browsers tab. Select a browser/ version and click OK twice.

Four at least of these programs are leaders in their respective fields. The point about Office, however, is that it integrates the four modules exceptionally well. With the exception of Outlook, which has to adopt a relatively individualistic approach, the modules share a common look and feel. (See Chapter 7 for more on how to integrate the Office modules.)

The illustration below shows the Word opening screen. Flagged are components which are also common to PowerPoint, Access, Outlook and Excel. (There are also differences between the module screens: Outlook, for instance, because of its very different nature, has fewer toolbars. We'll explore this in later chapters.)

Title bar   Menu bar   Toolbar

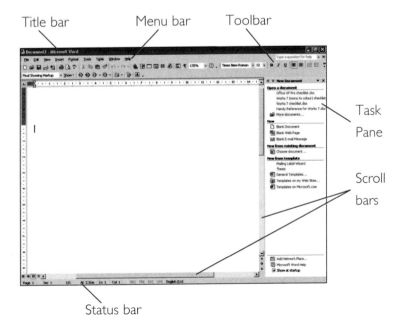

Task Pane

Scroll bars

Status bar

Toolbars

To add a new button to a toolbar, right-click over the toolbar. Click Customize. In the dialog which launches, click the Commands tab. In the Categories field, click a category (a group of associated icons). In the Commands box, drag a button onto the toolbar in the open document. Click Close.

Toolbars are important components in all five Office XP Professional modules. A toolbar is an on-screen bar which contains shortcut buttons. These symbolize and allow easy access to often-used commands which would normally have to be invoked via one or more menus.

For example, Word 2002's Standard toolbar lets you:

- create, open, save and print documents

- perform copy & paste and cut & paste operations

- undo editing actions

- insert a hyperlink

by simply clicking on the relevant button.

Toolbars vary to some extent from module to module. We'll be looking at these in more detail as we encounter them. For the moment, some general advice:

Specifying which toolbars are displayed
In any Office module, pull down the View menu and click Toolbars. Now do the following:

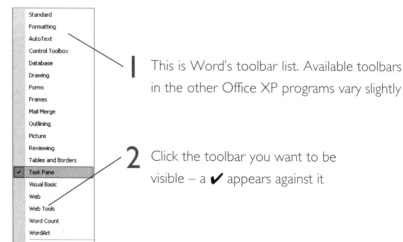

1 This is Word's toolbar list. Available toolbars in the other Office XP programs vary slightly

The Task Pane is a toolbar. To hide or show it, uncheck or check the Task Pane entry on the right.

2 Click the toolbar you want to be visible – a ✔ appears against it

Repeat this procedure for as many toolbars as necessary.

Automatic customization

Until Office 2000, it was true that, although different users use different features, no allowance had been made for this: the same features displayed on everyone's menus and toolbars...

Now, however, menus and toolbars are personalized in Office XP modules.

Personalized menus

When you first use a module, its menus display the features which Microsoft believes are used 95% of the time. Features which are infrequently used are not immediately visible. This is made clear in the illustrations below:

Office XP menus expand automatically, after a slight delay. However, to expand them manually, click the chevrons at the bottom of the menu.

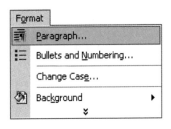

Word 2002's Format menu, as it first appears...

Automatic customization also applies to toolbars. Note the following:

- *if possible, they display on a single row*
- *they overlap when there isn't enough room on-screen*
- *icons are "promoted" and "demoted" like menu entries*
- *demoted icons are shown in a separate fly-out, reached by clicking:*

...the expanded menu. (As you use the modules, individual features are dynamically promoted or demoted. This means menus are continually evolving)

Creating new documents

With the exception of Outlook (Chapter 4) and Access (Chapter 6), all Office XP modules let you:

- create new blank documents

- create new documents based on a "template"

- create new documents with the help of a "Wizard"

Access 2002 only lets you create blank documents or documents based on wizards.

Because Word 2002, PowerPoint 2002, Excel 2002 and Access 2002 are more or less uniform in the way they create new documents, we'll look at this topic here rather than in the later chapters, which are specific to each program.

(However, see Chapter 5 for specialized advice on creating new slide shows, and Chapter 6 for more detail on creating databases.)

Blank documents

Creating blank documents is the simplest route to new document creation; use this if you want to define the document components yourself from scratch. This is often not the most efficient or effective way to create new documents.

Templates

Templates – also known as boilerplates – are sample documents complete with the relevant formatting and/or text. By basing a new document on a template, you automatically have access to these.

Wizards

Wizards are advanced templates which incorporate a question-and-answer system. You work through a series of dialogs, answering the appropriate questions and making the relevant choices.

Documents created with the use of templates or Wizards can easily be amended subsequently.

Both templates and Wizards are high-powered yet easy to use shortcuts to document creation. Office XP provides a large number of templates and Wizards.

Launching the New dialog

You can launch the New dialog via the Task Pane in any of the Office modules except Outlook.

| In Word 2002, Excel 2002, PowerPoint 2002 or Access 2002, refer to the Task Pane on the right of the screen and do the following:

Re step 2 – in Access, you must also go on to create a new table. In the Access-specific dialog, select Create table by entering data then enter your own data. Alternatively, select Create table by using wizard and use the wizard.

(For how to do both, see Chapter 6).

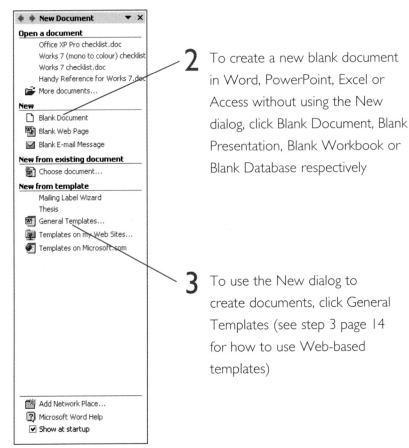

2 To create a new blank document in Word, PowerPoint, Excel or Access without using the New dialog, click Blank Document, Blank Presentation, Blank Workbook or Blank Database respectively

3 To use the New dialog to create documents, click General Templates (see step 3 page 14 for how to use Web-based templates)

4 Alternatively, click the Start button then All Programs, New Office Document (or Start, New Office Document in pre-XP versions of Windows) to launch the New dialog

Using the New dialog

The form the New dialog takes depends, to some extent, on which method you use to launch it. If you invoke it by using the Start button, you get the full version which incorporates elements from Word, Excel, PowerPoint and Access. You can then choose which type of new document you want to create.

If, on the other hand, you call up the New dialog from within Word, Excel, PowerPoint or Access, you get an abbreviated form specific to the program.

Using the full New dialog

First launch the New dialog. Then do the following:

If you base a new document on a template, Office creates a detailed document with preset (editable) text and formatting. If you use a wizard, on the other hand, you get a succession of dialogs. Complete these as appropriate. The end result is the same as using a template: a feature-rich document you can edit as necessary.

1 Activate a tab   3 Preview templates and wizards

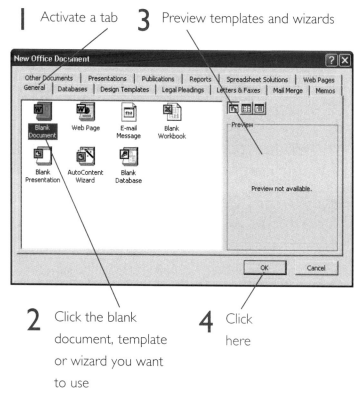

2 Click the blank document, template or wizard you want to use

4 Click here

5 Further dialogs may launch if you're using a template or wizard – complete these by following the on-screen instructions

Opening Office XP documents

For how to open existing contacts or tasks in Outlook 2002, see Chapter 4.

We saw earlier that Office XP lets you create new documents in various ways. You can also open Word 2002, Excel 2002, Access 2002 and PowerPoint 2002 documents you've already created.

In any module apart from Outlook, refer to the Task Pane on the right of the screen and perform steps 1–2 (if you haven't recently opened the relevant document, carry out steps 3–4 instead):

1 If your Task Pane is different, click the arrow and select New Document, New Workbook, New Presentation or New File

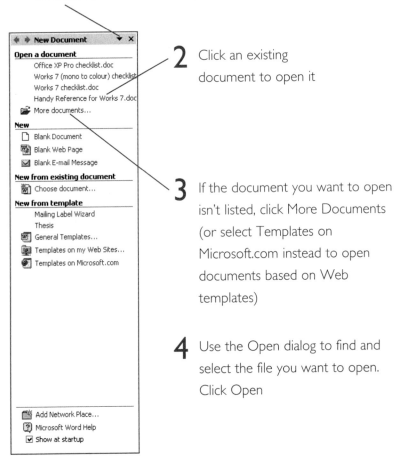

2 Click an existing document to open it

3 If the document you want to open isn't listed, click More Documents (or select Templates on Microsoft.com instead to open documents based on Web templates)

4 Use the Open dialog to find and select the file you want to open. Click Open

5 You can also launch the Open dialog directly from within any module except Outlook. Just press Ctrl+O

Opening Internet/Intranet files

From within any of the Office modules (apart from Outlook), you can open websites, Intranet sites or documents stored at FTP sites.

If the Web toolbar isn't currently on-screen, move the mouse pointer over any existing toolbar and right-click. In the menu which appears, click Web. Now do the following:

1 Ensure your Internet connection is live

 In Excel 2002, (providing you're using Internet Explorer 4.01 or higher) you can use these procedures to interact with Web-based spreadsheets.

For instance, you can enter data, create formulas, recalculate and sort/filter data and perform basic formatting, all directly from within the browser.

2 Click Go

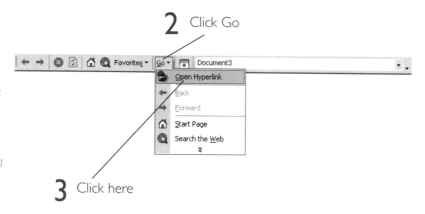

3 Click here

4 Type in the relevant address

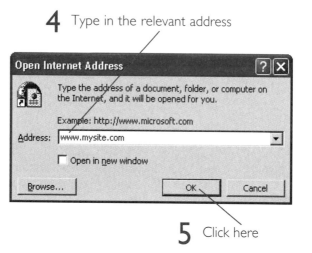

5 Click here

6 The Web/Intranet site selected in step 4 is opened in your browser

Saving Office XP documents

It's important to save your work at frequent intervals, in order to avoid data loss in the event of a hardware fault or power interruption. With the exception of Outlook, Office XP uses a consistent approach to saving.

Saving a document for the first time

In Word, Excel or PowerPoint, pull down the File menu and click Save. Or press Ctrl+S. Now do the following:

Access 2002 saves data automatically (e.g. when you open a record or close a datasheet or form). To perform a manual save, however, press Ctrl+S.

2 Click here then select a drive/folder combination in the drop-down list. Or click any buttons on the left for access to the relevant folders

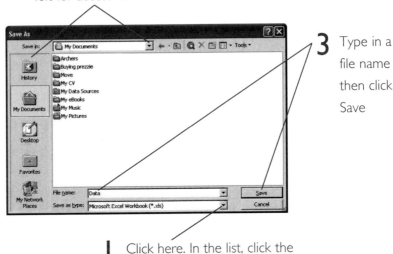

3 Type in a file name then click Save

Click here. In the list, click the format you want to save to

Saving previously saved documents

In Word 2002, you can use a special wizard to create Web pages. In the Task Pane, click General Templates. In the New dialog, select the Web Pages tab. Double-click Web Page Wizard and follow the on-screen instructions.

In Word, Excel or PowerPoint, pull down the File menu and click Save. Or press Ctrl+S. No dialog launches; instead, Office XP saves the latest version of your document to disk, overwriting the previous version.

Saving to the Internet

To create a shortcut to a Web/FTP folder, you must have a live Internet connection, rights to view/save files and its URL.

To create a shortcut to an Intranet folder, you must have a network connection, rights to view/save files and its network address.

In any of the Office XP modules (apart from Access and Outlook), you can save documents (usually in HTML – HyperText Markup Language – format) to network, Web or FTP servers. You can do this so long as you've created a shortcut to the folder that contains them.

Creating shortcuts to Web/FTP folders

| Open the Word, Excel or PowerPoint Open or Save As dialog and do the following:

3 Double-click Add Network Place

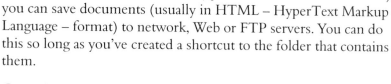

Creating shortcuts to local network folders requires a different procedure.

Windows 2000/Me/XP users should use My Network Places, while Windows NT 4.0 and 98 users should use Network Neighborhood. (For how to do this, see your system administrator.)

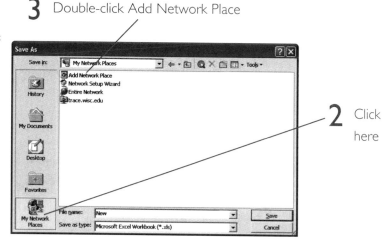

2 Click here

Saving to the Internet in Access 2002 is more complex – see pages 207–210 for more information.

4 Complete the Add Network Place wizard

Saving to shortcuts

| Pull down the File menu and click Save As Web Page. In Word, click in the Save as type: field and select Web Page or Web Page, Filtered (the final option strips out most Word-specific formatting and produces much smaller file sizes); in Excel or PowerPoint, select Web Page. Complete the rest of the dialog in the normal way then select a destination shortcut and a destination format. Click OK

Editing in Internet Explorer

When you create HTML files from within Office XP modules (see below), they can be edited from within Internet Explorer 5.x or later. This means that Office files, converted to HTML format and saved to the Web, can be run by the majority of Internet users.

Look at the illustration below:

See Chapter 5 for how to run slide shows in Internet Explorer itself.

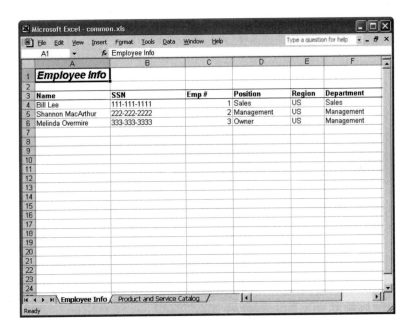

This is a simple Excel 2002 worksheet. You can use the techniques discussed on page 17 to convert it to a HTML file – see "Saving to shortcuts". Once the HTML file has been opened in Internet Explorer, do the following:

You may not be able to accurately edit HTML files in Internet Explorer if they were created in Word with the Filtered HTML export option – see page 17.

1 Click the toolbar Edit icon (its precise form reflects the original Office module):

2 After step 1, the file is opened within the originating Office module, with the formatting intact despite the "round-trip". Use standard editing techniques to make the relevant amendments

Saving configuration settings

You could save configuration details on your website, as a handy backup.

You can use a special wizard – the Save My Settings Wizard – to save configuration details in a special file (with the extension .ops). You can then restore the details in the file as a way of transferring your Office XP settings to another machine, or as a backup for your existing PC.

Using the Save My Settings Wizard

1 Close all Office programs (not doing so can result in faulty configuration details being written)

2 Click Start, Programs, Microsoft Office Tools, Save My Settings Wizard

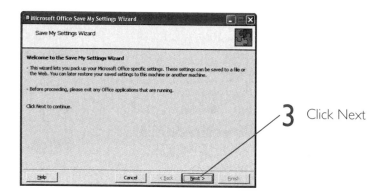

3 Click Next

4 Click Save... to save configuration details, or Restore... to implement previously saved settings

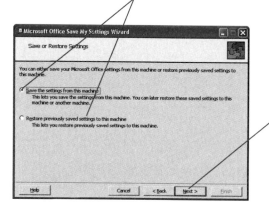

5 Click Next and complete the subsequent dialogs

Ask-a-Question

Office XP has the standard, Windows-style Help features. It also has something called Ask-a-Question.

In Office 2000, users had to run the Office Assistant (see the tip) to get answers to plain-English questions. In Office XP, however, this isn't the case. Simply do the following:

The Office Assistant is turned off by default. To turn it on, pull down the Help menu and click Show Office Assistant.

The Assistant is an animated (and frequently unpopular) helper which answers questions, but you can achieve the same effect more easily with Ask-a-Question.

Type in your question here and press Enter

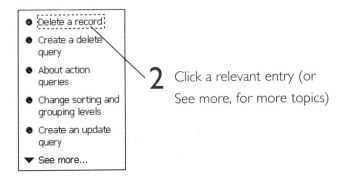

2 Click a relevant entry (or See more, for more topics)

3 Standard Office Help now launches – select the correct topic

The Shortcut bar – an overview

The main function of the Windows Taskbar is to switch between already open applications. However, it doesn't let you start programs directly with a single click on a button (instead, you have to use the normal Start menu route, which requires several clicks and/or mouse movements). The Office Shortcut bar rectifies this omission. You can add buttons for any programs you want, and start them very quickly and easily.

The Shortcut bar also mimics the Taskbar, but with one important difference. If a program is already open, clicking on its button on the Shortcut bar switches to it and also opens a new blank window. (This only works with Office XP programs; if you try it with other applications, a second copy launches instead.)

You can determine the Shortcut bar's on-screen location. Additionally, you can have it display permanently, or "auto-hide" it (where it only appears on screen when you move the mouse pointer to a specific screen area).

Toolbars

Buttons on the Shortcut bar are organized into specialist *toolbars*. The main ones are:

Office	has buttons relating specifically to Office XP modules
Programs	has buttons representing program folders
Desktop	has buttons representing items on your Desktop (e.g. My Computer, Internet Explorer and Recycle Bin)
Accessories	has buttons representing programs normally accessed from the Start/Accessories menu (e.g. Notepad, WordPad and Paint)
Favorites	has links to Web (and other) sites you've designated as Favorites

You can display as many, or as few, toolbars as you want.

Displaying Shortcut bar toolbars

Office uses a unique effect when you have more than one toolbar displayed at once on the Shortcut bar: it *layers* them.

Look at the illustration below:

Here, the Shortcut bar is "floating"; for how to display it on the top, bottom, left or right (the default) of your screen instead, see the facing page.

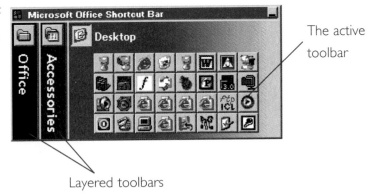

The active toolbar

Layered toolbars

To make another toolbar active, simply left-click on it (if the Shortcut bar is on the edge of the screen, right-click the active toolbar and select a new one in the contextual menu).

Hiding/revealing toolbars

To display a toolbar, move the mouse pointer over the Shortcut bar and right-click once. Now do the following:

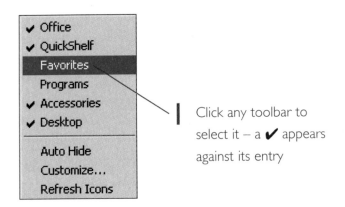

Click any toolbar to select it – a ✔ appears against its entry

2 Click any checked entry to deselect it

Specifying the Shortcut bar location

You can have the Shortcut bar display on the left or right, or on the top or bottom of your screen. Alternatively, you can have it "float" on screen, as a separate window. Use whichever method is most convenient for the task in hand.

Positioning the Shortcut bar on the screen edge

To move the Shortcut bar to the top, bottom, left or right of your screen (Office calls this "docking"), place the mouse pointer anywhere over the Shortcut bar (but not over one of the buttons). Drag the bar to the appropriate area. When you release the button, the bar "docks" automatically.

The Shortcut bar docked horizontally over PowerPoint

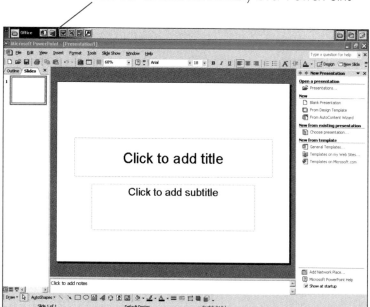

Restoring the Shortcut bar to its previous location

Double-click its Title bar (or drag the bar off the screen edge)

Auto-hiding the Shortcut bar

When it's floating, the Shortcut bar behaves much like any other window. For example, if it's minimized, clicking on the Shortcut bar button on the Taskbar maximizes it.

If it's docked, though, the Shortcut bar can be made to conceal itself when not required (this is called Auto-Hide).

| Double-click in the Shortcut bar (but not on a button or in the Title bar)

You can also use a shortcut to Auto-Hide the Shortcut bar. Right-click over the bar; in the menu which appears, click Auto Hide.

Uncheck Always on Top if you don't want the Shortcut bar to have priority over all other windows.

2 Ensure the View tab is active

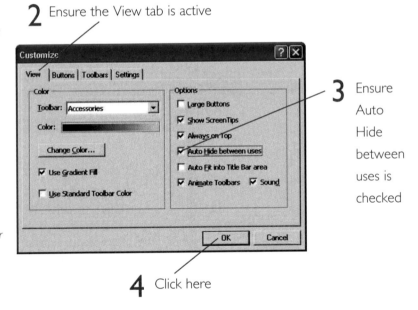

3 Ensure Auto Hide between uses is checked

4 Click here

5 If the Shortcut bar is floating (not docked), Auto-Hide has no immediate effect on it

Making the Shortcut bar reappear temporarily

To make the Shortcut bar visible again when you need it, simply move the mouse pointer to the edge of the screen where the Office Shortcut bar is docked. For instance, if the bar was docked on the bottom of the screen, move the pointer as far down as it will go.

When you've finished, move the mouse pointer away from the docking area; the Shortcut bar disappears again.

Adding buttons to the Shortcut bar

You can add buttons that represent files (program files, or just about any other kind of file) or folders to the Shortcut bar.

Double-click in the Shortcut bar (but not on a button, or in the Title bar). Now do the following:

1 Ensure this tab is active then select a toolbar

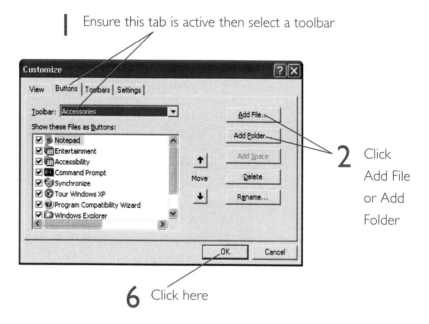

2 Click Add File or Add Folder

6 Click here

3 Click here. In the drop-down list, click the relevant drive/folder combination

If, as here, you add a button representing a graphic file, clicking it will start whichever application is associated with the file type, and the file will open in it.

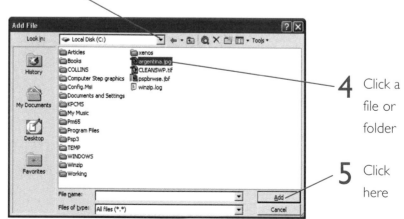

4 Click a file or folder

5 Click here

Quick File Switching

In order to use Quick File Switching you need to be using Windows 98 or later, or Windows 95 with Internet Explorer 4.0 (or a later version).

In the past, only programs (not individual windows within programs) displayed on the Windows Taskbar. With Office XP, however, all open windows display as separate buttons.

In the following example, four new documents have been created in Word 2002. All four display as separate windows, although only one copy of Word 2002 is running:

Four Word 2002 windows

This is clarified by a glance at Word 2002's Window menu which (as before) shows all open Word windows:

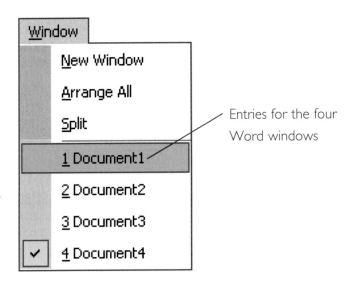

Entries for the four Word windows

Use this technique to go to a document window by simply clicking its Taskbar button, a considerable saving in time and effort.

Repairing errors

Office XP provides a special feature you can use to repair damage to modules.

Detect and Repair

Do the following to correct program errors (but note selecting Discard my customized settings and restore default settings in step 2 will ensure that all default Office settings are restored, so any you've customized – including menu/toolbar positions, new Shortcut Bar buttons and view settings – will be lost):

1 In any module, pull down the Help menu and select Detect and Repair

2 Select one or both options

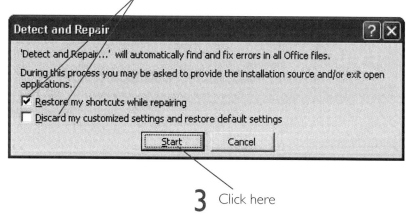

Detect and Repair

'Detect and Repair...' will automatically find and fix errors in all Office files.

During this process you may be asked to provide the installation source and/or exit open applications.

☑ Restore my shortcuts while repairing
☐ Discard my customized settings and restore default settings

Start   Cancel

3 Click here

In Word and Excel, you can use another method to repair damaged files. Press Ctrl+O. In the open dialog, highlight the corrupt file and click the drop-down arrow on the Open button. In the menu, click Open and Repair.

(Word and Excel may run this procedure automatically when errors are detected.)

4 Follow the on-screen instructions – Detect and Repair can be a lengthy process

5 You may have to re-enter your user name and initials when you restart your Office applications

...cont'd

You can also use a further procedure for instances when an Office module "hangs" (ceases to respond).

Application Recovery

When errors occur, Word, Excel, Access and PowerPoint should give you the option of saving open files before the application closes.

| Click Start, Programs, Microsoft Office Tools, Microsoft Office Application Recovery

2 Select the program which isn't responding

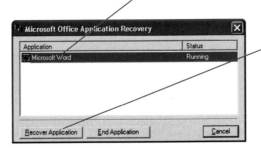

3 Click Recover Application to have Office try to recover the file(s) you were working on

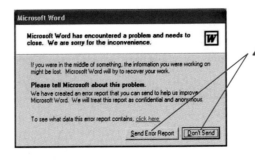

4 Select Send Error Report to email error details to Microsoft, or Don't Send

Files with [Recovered] against them are usually more recent than those with [Original] in the title.

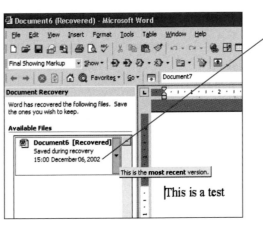

5 The module opens. Click the file you want to keep (usually the most recent) then select Open or View to view it or Save As to save it

This is the Document Recovery Task Pane – when you've finished with it, click the Close button.

Collect and Paste

Using Office XP, if you want to copy-and-paste multiple items of text and/or pictures into a document, you can now copy as many as 24 items. These are stored in a special version of the Windows Clipboard called the Office Clipboard, which in turn is located in the Task Pane. The Office Clipboard displays a visual representation of the data.

Using the Office Clipboard

From within Word, Excel, PowerPoint, Access or Outlook, use standard procedures to copy multiple examples of text and/or pictures – after the first copy, the Clipboard should appear in the Task Pane. Do the following, in the same or another module:

1 Click the data you want to insert – it appears at the insertion point

To call up the Office Clipboard at any time, pull down the Edit menu and click Office Clipboard.

Copying items bigger than 4Mb (with up to 64 Mb of RAM) or 8Mb (with more than 64Mb) to the Office Clipboard will mean it can accept no further data.

2 If you're inserting text, a Smart Tag appears – see Chapter 2

3 To clear the contents of the Office XP Clipboard, click the Clear All button

Office's Task Pane

The New Document Task Pane is called the New Workbook, New Presentation and New File Task Pane in Excel, PowerPoint and Access respectively. (It's also slightly different in each.)

Office XP modules provide a special pane on the right of the screen which you can use to launch various tasks or apply formatting. There are various incarnations of the Task Pane. For example, Word 2002 has eight, of which the main ones are:

- New Document (see page 14)

- Clipboard (see page 29)

- Search (see Chapter 2)

- Insert Clip Art (see Chapter 2)

Using the Task Pane

To display or hide the Task Pane, pull down the View menu and click Task Pane. (In Access, however, click Toolbars, Task Pane)

2 To select a new Task Pane, click here – in the menu, click an entry

3 Click here to launch Office XP's Help system

Digital signatures

You can attach digital signatures to Office XP documents, as a way of enhancing security. The signature confirms that the document was sent by you and hasn't been altered in any way, and uses a digital certificate.

Creating digital certificates

| Locate a file called SELFCERT.EXE (usually in the C:\Program Files\Microsoft Office\Office10\ folder)

You can also obtain digital certificates from commercial companies. For more information, visit:

http://officeupdate. microsoft.com/office/redirect/ fromOffice9/cert. htm

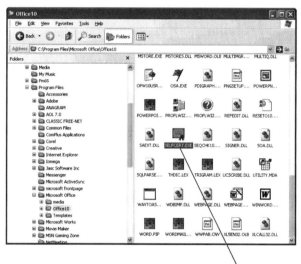

Running the procedure here creates a self-certification. Self-certification doesn't carry the weight of certification by a formal certification authority (see the above tip).

2 In My Computer, double-click SELFCERT.EXE

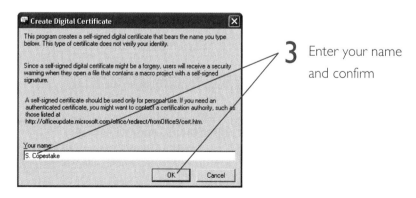

3 Enter your name and confirm

...cont'd

Applying digital signatures

If you're using Office as a member of an organization, it may have its own certification authority. Contact your network administrator or IT department for more information.

1 In Word, Excel or PowerPoint, pull down the Tools menu and click Options (you can only apply signatures to saved files)

2 Click the Security tab

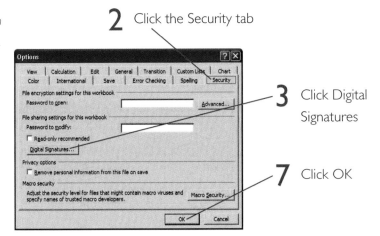

3 Click Digital Signatures

7 Click OK

4 Click Add

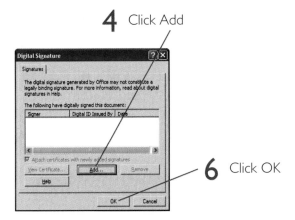

6 Click OK

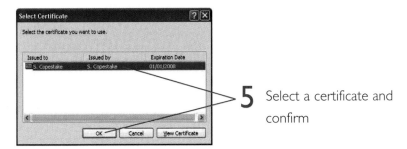

5 Select a certificate and confirm

Word 2002

Here, you'll become familiar with basic/advanced Word use. You'll enter/select text, send email and use Smart Tags. You'll format text, translate it and use styles. Finally, you'll proof/summarize your work; create bookmarks/hyperlinks; insert images, backgrounds and watermarks; and customize page layout/printing.

Covers

Chapter Two

The Word 2002 screen

Below is a detailed illustration of the Word 2002 screen:

Title bar　　　Menu bar　　　Toolbars

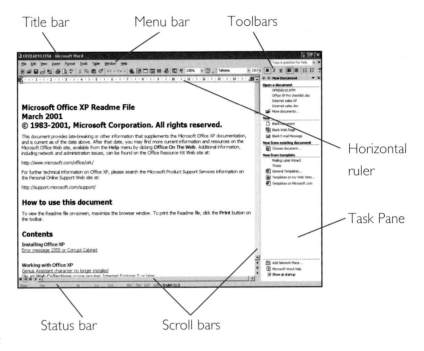

Horizontal ruler

Task Pane

Status bar　　　Scroll bars

The Status bar displays information relating to the active document (e.g. what page you're on).

Some of these – e.g. the rulers and scroll bars – are standard to just about all programs that run under Windows. Many of them can be hidden, if required.

Specifying which screen components display

Pull down the Tools menu and click Options. Then:

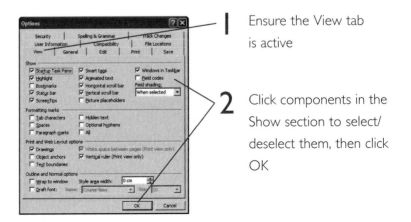

I Ensure the View tab is active

2 Click components in the Show section to select/ deselect them, then click OK

Entering text

You can also use Click and Type to enter text almost anywhere in a document, without inserting the necessary paragraph marks or formatting – see pages 37–38.

Word 2002 lets you enter text immediately after you've started it (you can do this because a new blank document is automatically created based on the default template). In Word, you enter text at the insertion point:

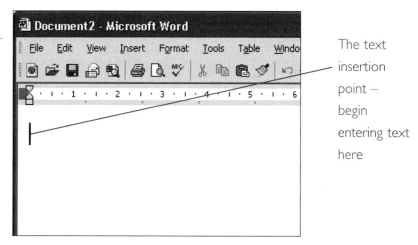

The text insertion point – begin entering text here

You can have Word 2002 insert words or phrases for you.
Place the insertion point where you want the text inserted. Pull down the Insert menu and click AutoText. In the sub-menu, click a category (e.g. Salutation) then a glossary entry; Word inserts the entry.

Additional characters

Most of the text you need to enter can be typed in directly from the keyboard. However, it's sometimes necessary to enter special characters, e.g. bullets (for instance: ✍) or special symbols like ©.

Pull down the Insert menu and click Symbol. Do the following:

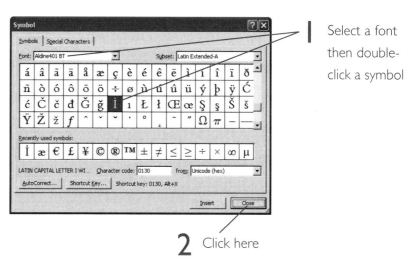

1 Select a font then double-click a symbol

2 Click here

Selecting text

Word 2002 supports standard Windows text selection techniques. However, it also supports the following:

Selecting partial text blocks

To select a rectangular part of 1 or more paragraphs, hold down Alt as you drag

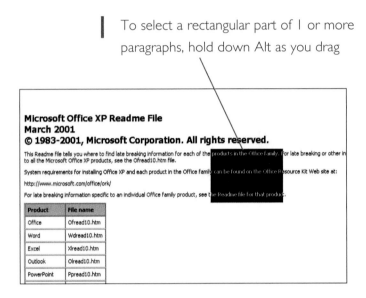

Selecting multiple text blocks

To select more than 1 text block, hold down Ctrl+Shift as you drag with the mouse

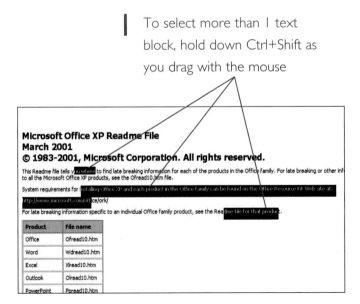

Click and Type

You can also enter text in a special way in Word 2002, one that makes the process much easier. With Click and Type:

- you can enter text or pictures in most blank page areas, with the minimum of mouse activity

- you don't have to apply the necessary formatting yourself – Word 2002 does this automatically (e.g. you can insert text to the right of an existing paragraph without having to insert manual tab stops)

Using Click and Type

In Web Layout or Print Layout view, position the mouse pointer where you want to insert text or a picture. Click once – the pointer changes to indicate the formatting which Word 2002 will apply:

If Click and Type isn't enabled, pull down the Tools menu and click Options. In the Options dialog, activate the Edit tab. In the Click and type section, check Enable click and type. Click OK.

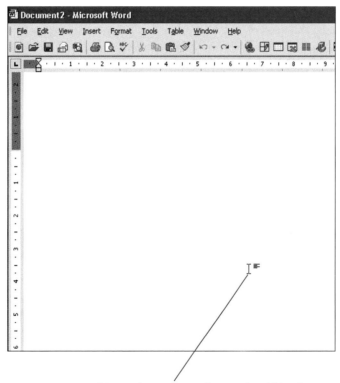

Here, the pointer shows that Word 2002 is about to left-align new text...

Now double-click, then do the following:

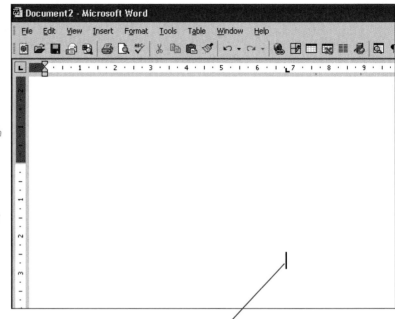

If you use Click and Type beneath an existing text paragraph, Word 2002 applies a specific style to the new text. You can specify the style used.

Pull down the Tools menu and click Options. In the Options dialog, activate the Edit tab. In the Click and type section, click in the Default paragraph style field. In the drop-down list, select a style. Finally, click OK.

Begin entering text, or insert a picture in the normal way

The Click and Type pointers

The main pointers are:

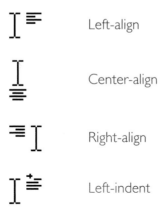

Left-align

Center-align

Right-align

Left-indent

Using Smart Tags

Word 2002 recognizes certain types of data and underlines them with a dotted purple underline or a small blue box. When you move the mouse pointer over the line/box an "action button" appears which provides access to commands which would otherwise have to be accessed from menus/toolbars or other programs.

The Paste Options button

| "Button" has been copied and the Paste command (Shift+Insert) issued...

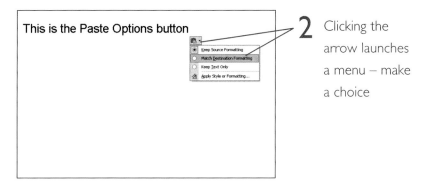

This is the Paste Options button

2 Clicking the arrow launches a menu – make a choice

The AutoCorrect button

| An AutoCorrect entry has been set up which replaces "bu" with "button"

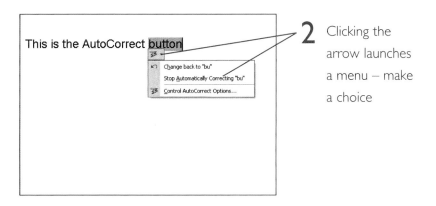

This is the AutoCorrect button

2 Clicking the arrow launches a menu – make a choice

Sending email

You can use Word to write and send email messages (provided you've also installed Outlook).

In the New Document Task Pane, click General Templates. In the New dialog, activate the General tab. Double-click the E-mail Message icon. Now do the following:

To send email from Word, you must have specified Outlook 2002 as your Internet email program.

Within Internet Explorer, click Internet Options in the Tools menu. Click the Programs tab. In the E-mail field, select Microsoft Outlook. Click OK.

1 Type in the recipient's email address

2 Type in a subject

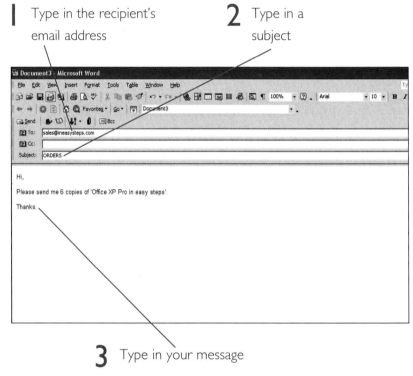

3 Type in your message

4 Click the Send button in the toolbar

You may have to configure Outlook 2002's Remote Mail facility before you can send email. See Chapter 4.

Emailing a pre-written document

1 Click this button in Word's Standard toolbar:

2 Follow steps 1, 2 and 4 above

Moving around in documents

To move to the location where you last made an amendment, press Shift+F5. You can do this as many as three times in succession.

You can use the following to move through Word 2002 documents:

- keystrokes

- the vertical/horizontal scroll bars

- the Go To section of the Find and Replace dialog

The keystroke route

Word implements the standard Windows direction keys. Use the left, right, up and down cursor keys in the usual way. Additionally, Home, End, Page Up and Page Down work normally.

The scroll bar route

Use your mouse to perform any of the following actions:

The yellow box to the left of the vertical scroll bar is the Page Indicator. When you drag the box on the scroll bar, the Page Indicator shows which page you're up to (it doesn't appear in Web Layout view.)

Click anywhere here to jump to another location in the document

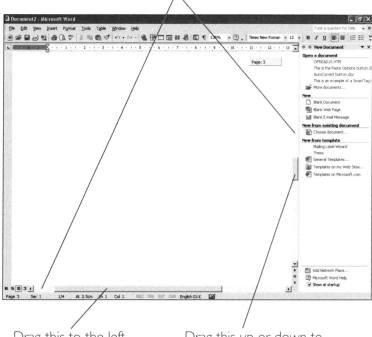

Drag this to the left or right to extend the viewing area

Drag this up or down to move through the active document

The dialog route

You can use the Go To tab in the Find and Replace dialog to move to a variety of document locations. These include:

- pages (probably the most common)

- lines

- pictures

Pull down the Edit menu and click Go To (or press the F5 key). Now do the following:

To have Word count the words in the active document, pull down the Tools menu and click Word Count.

Click the location type you want to go to

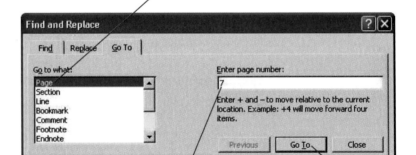

2 Type in the specific location reference (e.g. a number if you selected "Page" in step 1)

3 Click here

There are some useful refinements:

- You can enter *relative* movements in step 2. For example, if you want to move seventeen pages back from the present location, type in -17. Or +5 to move five pages forward...

- To move to the next or previous instance of the specified location (i.e. without specifying a reference), omit step 2. In step 3, the dialog is now slightly different; click Next or Previous, as appropriate. Click Close when you've finished

Views

Word 2002 lets you examine your work in various ways, according to the approach you need. It calls these "views". The principal views are:

Normal

Normal View – the default – is used for basic text editing. In Normal View, text formatting elements are still visible; for instance, colored, emboldened or italicized text displays faithfully. However, little attempt is made to show document structure or layout (for example, headers/footers, page boundaries and most pictures are invisible).

For these reasons, Normal View is quick and easy to use. It's suitable for bulk text entry and editing, but not recommended for use with graphics.

Print Layout

Print Layout view works like Normal view, with one exception: the positioning of items on the page is reproduced accurately. Headers/footers and pictures are visible, and can be edited directly; margins display faithfully.

In Print Layout view, the screen is updated more slowly. Use it when your document is nearing completion.

Hiding white space

You can hide blank (unused) space in Print Layout view:

1 Move the mouse pointer over the top or bottom of the page – two white arrows appear:

2 Click to toggle between hiding and displaying white space

Web Layout

In Web layout view, Web pages are optimized so that they appear as they will when published to the Web or an Intranet. Effects which are often used on the Web display (e.g. backgrounds and AutoShapes).

When Full Screen view is active, you lose access to toolbars and scroll bars. However, you should still be able to access the menus by using the keyboard (e.g. Alt+F to launch the File menu).

Full Screen

Unless you have a particularly large monitor, you'll probably find that there are times when your screen is too cluttered. Full Screen view hides all standard screen components in one operation, thereby making more space available for editing.

Use Full Screen view when you need it.

To switch to another view, pull down the View menu and select one.

| To leave Full Screen view, press Esc or click the Close Full Screen button

Summarizing documents

In effect, Word provides another way to view a document: you can "summarize" it. When you summarize a document, Word 2002:

*   analyses it and allocates a "score" to each sentence

*   allocates a higher score for sentences with repeated words

After this, you specify what percentage of the higher-scoring sentences you want to display.

To summarize the active document, pull down the Tools menu and click AutoSummarize. Word 2002 carries out the initial analysis. When it's completed, do the following:

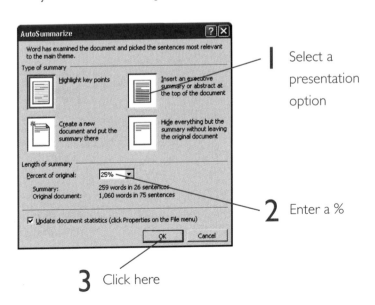

| Select a presentation option

2 Enter a %

3 Click here

Changing zoom levels

The ability to vary the level of magnification for the active document is often useful. Sometimes, it's helpful to "zoom out" (i.e. decrease the magnification) so that you can take an overview; at other times, you'll need to "zoom in" (increase it) to work in greater detail. Word 2002 lets you do either of these very easily.

You can do any of the following:

• choose from preset zoom levels (e.g. 100%, 75%)

• specify your own zoom percentage

• choose Many Pages, to view a specific number of pages

Setting the zoom level

Pull down the View menu and click Zoom. Now carry out steps 1 or 2 (to specify a zoom %) OR 3 & 4 (to specify a group of pages). Finally, in either case, follow step 5.

The Zoom dialog varies slightly according to which view you're using.

Click a preset zoom level

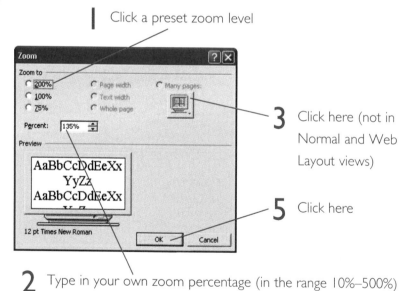

3 Click here (not in Normal and Web Layout views)

5 Click here

2 Type in your own zoom percentage (in the range 10%–500%)

1 x 2 Pages

4 Click a multiple-page view

Formatting text – an overview

Word 2002 lets you format text in a variety of ways. Broadly, however, text formatting can be divided into two overall categories:

You can format the active document automatically. Pull down the Tools menu and click AutoCorrect. In the AutoCorrect dialog, click the AutoFormat tab. Specify the type(s) of formatting you want applied. Finally, click OK.

Character formatting

Character formatting is concerned with altering the *appearance* of selected text. Examples include:

- changing the font and type size

- coloring text

- changing the font style (bold, italic etc.)

- underlining text

- applying font effects (superscript, subscript, small caps etc.)

Character formatting is a misnomer in one sense: it can also be applied to specific paragraphs of text.

Whenever you type in Internet addresses AutoFormat automatically implements them as hypertext links.

(To turn this feature off, pull down the Tools menu and select AutoCorrect Options. In the dialog, select the AutoFormat As You Type tab. Uncheck Internet and network paths with hyperlinks. Click OK.)

Paragraph formatting

Paragraph formatting has to do with the structuring and layout of paragraphs of text. Examples include:

- specifying paragraph indents

- specifying paragraph alignment (e.g. left or right justification)

- specifying paragraph and line spacing

- imposing borders and/or fills on paragraphs

The term "paragraph formatting" is also something of a misnomer in that some of these – for instance, line-spacing – can also be applied to the whole of the active document rather than selected paragraphs.

Changing the font or type size

Character formatting can be changed in two ways.

Applying a new font/type size – the dialog route
First, select the text whose typeface and/or type size you want to amend. Pull down the Format menu and click Font. Now carry out step 1. Perform step 2 and/or 3. Finally, carry out step 4:

| Ensure the Font tab is active

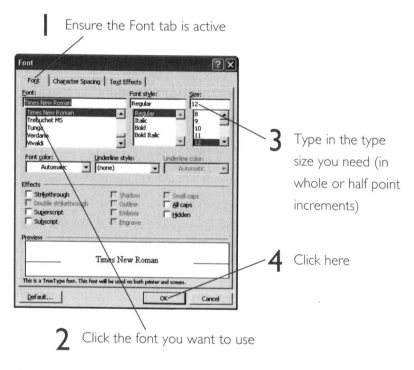

3 Type in the type size you need (in whole or half point increments)

4 Click here

2 Click the font you want to use

If the Formatting toolbar isn't currently visible, pull down the View menu and click Toolbars, Formatting.

Applying a new font/type size – the toolbar route
Make sure the Formatting toolbar is visible. Now select the text you want to amend and do the following:

Click here; select the font you want to use in the drop-down list

Type in the type size you need and press Enter

Changing text color

You can also change font styles. The default is Regular. Extra font styles depend on the typeface. For example, Times New Roman has "Bold", "Italic" and "Bold Italic" while "Arial Rounded MT Bold" merely has "Bold" and "Bold Italic".

First, select the text you want to alter. Pull down the Format menu and click Font. Now do the following:

1 Ensure the Font tab is active

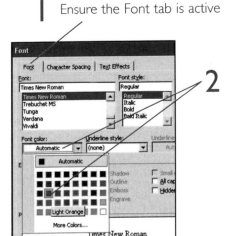

2 Click here, select a color then click OK (clicking Automatic sets the color to black, unless you've amended the default Windows text color)

Don't confuse font styles with text styles (text styles are groups of formatting commands and are much more diverse).

Verifying current text formatting

If you're unsure about what formatting attributes are associated with text, press Shift+F1. Now click in the text. This is the result:

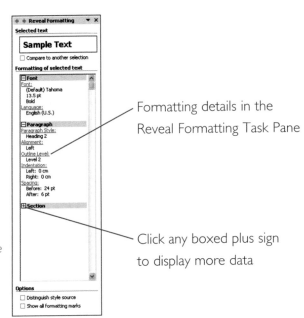

Formatting details in the Reveal Formatting Task Pane

Click any boxed plus sign to display more data

Select Show all formatting marks at the base of the Task Pane to display tabs, paragraph marks and spaces etc.

Font effects

You can also use the following handy keyboard shortcuts to apply effects:

Ctrl++	*Superscript*
Ctrl+=	*Subscript*
Ctrl+Shift+K	*Small Caps*
Ctrl+Shift+A	*All Caps*
Ctrl+Shift+H	*Hidden*

The following are the principal font effects:

* Strikethrough – e.g. ~~font effect~~

* Superscript – e.g. f$^{ont\ effect}$

* Subscript – e.g. f$_{ont\ effect}$

* All Caps – e.g. FONT EFFECT

* Small Caps – e.g. FONT EFFECT

In addition, you can mark text as hidden, which means that it doesn't display on screen or print.

Applying font effects

First, select the relevant text. Pull down the Format menu and click Font. Then carry out the following steps:

| Ensure the Font tab is active

Many of the font effects can be combined – e.g. Superscript with Small Caps. However, Small Caps and All Caps are mutually exclusive.

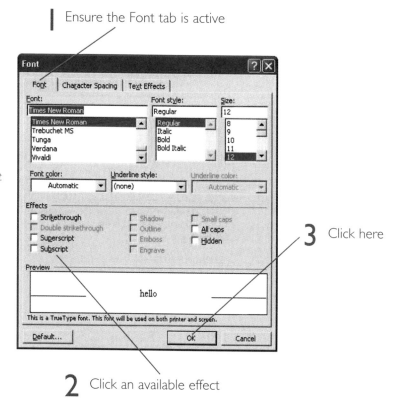

3 Click here

2 Click an available effect

Indenting text – an overview

You can achieve a similar effect by using tabs. However, indents are easier to apply (and amend subsequently).

Indents are a crucial component of document layout. For instance, in most document types, indenting the first line of paragraphs (i.e. moving it inwards away from the left page margin) makes the text much more legible.

Other document types – e.g. bibliographies – can use the following:

- negative indents (where the direction of indent is towards and beyond the left margin)

- hanging indents (where the first line is unaltered, while subsequent lines are indented)

- full indents (where the entire paragraph is indented away from the left and/or the right margins)

Some of the potential indent combinations are shown in the illustration below:

Don't confuse indents with page margins. Margins are the gap between the edge of the page and the text area; indents define the distance between the margins and text.

This paragraph has a full left and right indent. It's best, however, not to overdo the extent of the indent: 0.35 inches is often more than adequate.

Left & right indent

This paragraph has a first-line indent. This type of indent is suitable for most document types. It's best, however, not to overdo the extent of the indent: 0.35 inches is often more than adequate.

First-line indent

This paragraph has a negative left indent. It's best, however, not to overdo the extent of the indent: 0.35 inches is often more than adequate.

Negative left indent

This paragraph has a hanging indent. It's best, however, not to overdo the extent of the indent: 0.35 inches is often more than adequate.

Hanging indent

Left and right margins (inserted for illustration purposes)

Applying indents to paragraphs

Indenting text – the dialog route

Select the paragraph(s) you want to indent. Pull down the Format menu and click Paragraph. Follow step 1 below. If you want a left or right indent, carry out step 2. To achieve a first-line or hanging indent, follow step 3. Finally, carry out step 4.

1 Ensure the Indents and Spacing tab is active

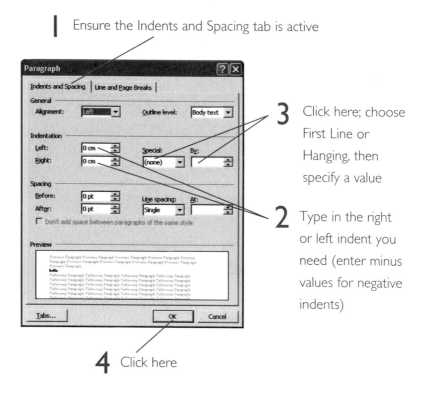

3 Click here; choose First Line or Hanging, then specify a value

2 Type in the right or left indent you need (enter minus values for negative indents)

4 Click here

Indenting text – the toolbar route

First, select the relevant paragraph(s). Ensure the Formatting toolbar is visible. Then click one of these:

Increases the indent

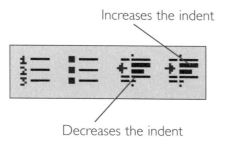

Decreases the indent

Aligning paragraphs

Word 2002 supports the following types of alignment:

Align Left — Text is flush with the left page margin.

Align Right — Text is flush with the right page margin.

Justify — Text is flush with the left *and* right page margins.

Center — Text is placed evenly between the left/ right page margins.

Aligning text – the dialog route

First, select the paragraph(s) you want to align. Pull down the Format menu and click Paragraph. Now:

Select the Indents and Spacing tab

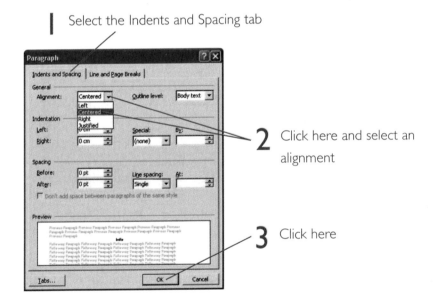

2 Click here and select an alignment

3 Click here

Aligning text – the toolbar route

Select the relevant paragraph(s). Then click one of these:

The Align Right or Justify icons may be hidden if you haven't used them recently.

Align Left   Justify

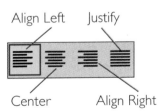

Center   Align Right

Specifying paragraph spacing

Word 2002 lets you customize the vertical space before and/or after specific text paragraphs. This is a useful device for increasing text legibility.

By default, Word defines paragraph spacing – like type sizes – in point sizes. However, if you want you can enter measurements in different units. To do this, apply any of the following suffixes to values you enter:

- in – for inches (e.g. "2 in")

You should find the following typographical/ computing definitions useful:

- cm – for centimeters (e.g. "5 cm")

- pi – for picas (e.g. "14 pi")

- Picas are an alternative measure in typography: one pica is almost equivalent to one-sixth inch. Picas are often used to define line length

- px – for pixels (e.g. "40 px" – about ½ inch)

- Pixels (a contraction of "picture elements") are the smallest components of the picture on a computer monitor

Applying paragraph spacing

First, select the relevant paragraph(s). Pull down the Format menu and click Paragraph. Now carry out the steps below:

| Ensure the Indents and Spacing tab is active

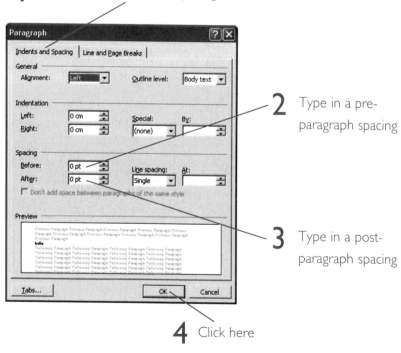

2 Type in a pre-paragraph spacing

3 Type in a post-paragraph spacing

4 Click here

Adjusting line spacing

Line spacing (also known as leading – pronounced "ledding") is the vertical distance between individual lines of text.

The standard line spacing is single. However, some types of writing require a non-standard line spacing. For example, fiction manuscripts are routinely presented with double line spacing, to aid emendation.

Types of line spacing supported by Word

You can apply the following types of leading:

Single
Each line of type is separated by an amount slightly greater than the type size. This is the default. Use Single for most writing types including letters.

1.5 Lines
150% of single line spacing.

Double
200% of single line spacing.

At Least
Sets the minimum line height at the value you specify.

Exactly
Sets the value you specify as an unvarying line height: Word 2002 cannot adjust it.

Multiple
Sets line height as a multiple of single-spaced text. (For example, specifying "3.5" here initiates a line height of 3.5 lines.)

Applying a new line spacing

1 Select the relevant paragraph(s)

2 Right-click the paragraph(s)

You can use these keyboard shortcuts to adjust line spacing:

Ctrl+1	*Single spacing*
Ctrl+5	*1 ½ spacing*
Ctrl+2	*Double spacing*

You can also use this technique to set the line spacing before you begin to enter text.

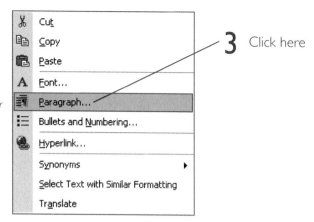

3 Click here

4 Perform step 5 below. If you want to apply a preset spacing, follow step 6. To implement your own spacing, carry out steps 7 and 8 instead. Finally, follow step 9:

5 Ensure the Indents and Spacing tab is active

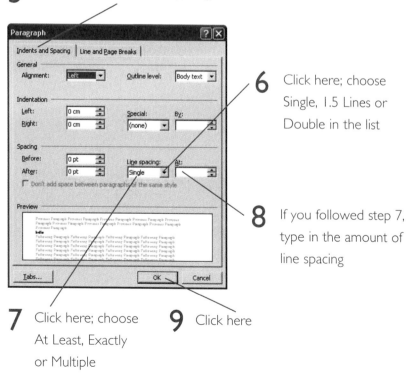

6 Click here; choose Single, 1.5 Lines or Double in the list

8 If you followed step 7, type in the amount of line spacing

7 Click here; choose At Least, Exactly or Multiple

9 Click here

Paragraph borders

By default, Word 2002 does not border paragraph text. However, you can apply a wide selection of borders if you want. You can specify:

You can also border selected text within a paragraph. However, the Borders tab is then slightly different (e.g. you can't deselect the border for specific sides).

- the type and thickness of the border

- how many sides the border should have

- the border color

- whether the text is shadowed or in 3-D

- the distance of the border from the text

Applying a border

First, select the paragraph(s) you want to border. Then pull down the Format menu and click Borders and Shading. Carry out step 1 below. Now carry out steps 2–5, as appropriate. Finally, perform step 6:

To set the distance from the border to the enclosed text, click Options. Insert the relevant distances and click OK. Then follow step 6.

I Ensure the Borders tab is active

4 Click a border option to border all four sides of the text

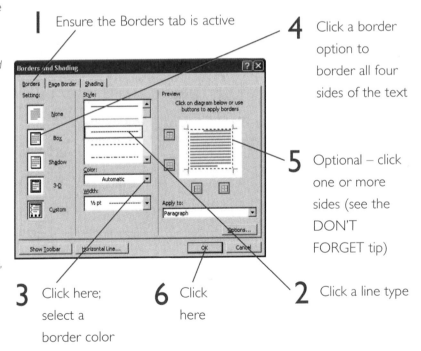

5 Optional – click one or more sides (see the DON'T FORGET tip)

Use step 5 to deselect the top, bottom, left or right paragraph borders. If you want to deselect more than one, repeat step 5 as often as necessary.

3 Click here; select a border color

6 Click here

2 Click a line type

Paragraph fills

By default, Word 2002 does not apply a fill to text paragraphs. However, you can do the following if you want:

- specify a percentage fill e.g. 20% (light grey) or 85% (very dark grey)

- apply a simple pattern, if required

- specify a background fill color

- specify a pattern color

Applying a fill

First, select the paragraph(s) you want to fill. Then pull down the Format menu and click Borders and Shading. Now carry out step 1 below. Follow steps 2, 3 or 4 as appropriate. Finally, carry out step 5:

1 Ensure the Shading tab is active

4 Click a background fill color

You can achieve unique blends by applying different pattern and background

colors.

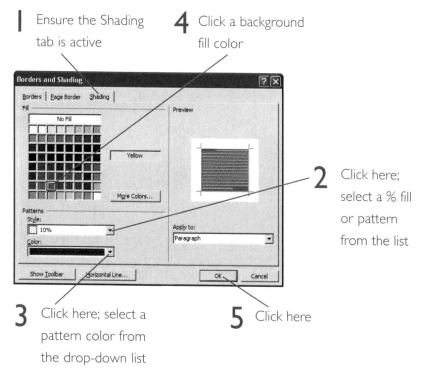

2 Click here; select a % fill or pattern from the list

3 Click here; select a pattern color from the drop-down list

5 Click here

Working with tabs

Tabs are a means of indenting the first line of text paragraphs (you can also use indents for this purpose – see pages 50–51).

When you press the Tab key while the text-insertion point is at the start of a paragraph, the text in the first line jumps to the next tab stop – see the illustration below:

Never use the Space Bar to indent paragraphs: spaces vary in size according to the typeface and type size applying to specific paragraphs, and therefore give uneven results.

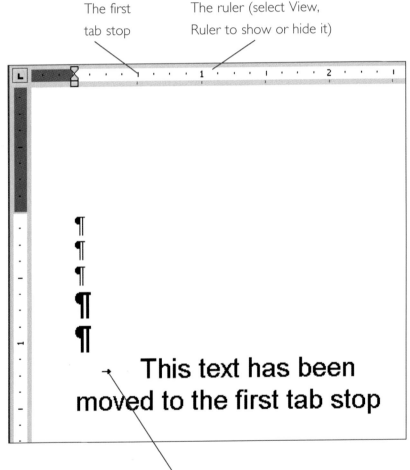

The first tab stop

The ruler (select View, Ruler to show or hide it)

This text has been moved to the first tab stop

To have tab stops (and other symbols) display, pull down the Tools menu and click Options. Activate the View tab, then select All in the Formatting marks section. Finally, click OK.

This arrow denotes the inserted tab

Inserting tabs is a useful way to increase the legibility of your text. By default, Word 2002 inserts tab stops automatically every half an inch. If you want, you can enter new or revised tab stop positions individually and with great precision.

Setting tab stops

1 Select the relevant paragraph(s)

2 Pull down the Format menu and click Tabs

3 Carry out step 4 below. If you want to implement a new default tab stop position, follow step 5. If, on the other hand, you need to set up individual tab stops, carry out steps 6 AND 7 as often as necessary. Finally, in either case, follow step 8 to confirm your changes:

To change the unit tabs are measured in, pull down the Tools menu and select Options. Activate the General tab then click in the Measurement units field and select a new one. Click OK.

5 Type in the new tab stop default

7 Click here

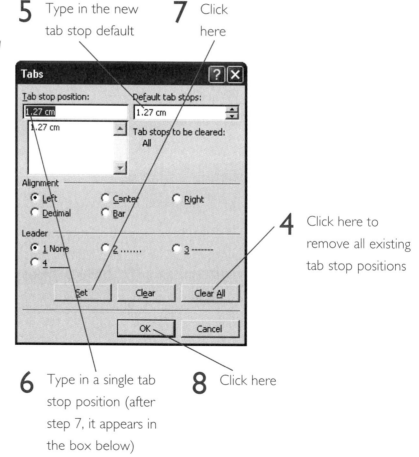

4 Click here to remove all existing tab stop positions

6 Type in a single tab stop position (after step 7, it appears in the box below)

8 Click here

Searching for text

Word 2002 lets you search for specific text within the active document. Even better, however, you can also search for character or paragraph formatting, either separately from the text search or at the same time.

For example, you can if you want have Word locate all instances of the word "information". Or you could have it find all italicized words, whatever they are. Similarly, you could have it flag all instances of "*information*".

You can also:

- limit the search to words which match the case of the text you specify (e.g. if you search for "Man", Word will not flag "man" or "MAN")

- limit the search to whole words (e.g. if you search for "nation", Word will not flag "international")

- have Word search for word forms (e.g. if you look for "began", Word will also stop at "begin", "begun" and "beginning")

- have Word search for homophones (e.g. if you look for "there", Word will flag "their")

To locate specific formatting, follow step 2. Then, in the extended dialog which launches, click Format. Word 2002 launches a menu; click the relevant entry. Complete the dialog which appears in the normal way. Finally, follow step 3 to begin the search.

Initiating a text search

Pull down the Edit menu and click Find. Now do the following:

To highlight all instances of the specified text, check Highlight all items found in. Select an area (e.g. Main Document) in the list then click Find All.

1 Type in the text you want to find

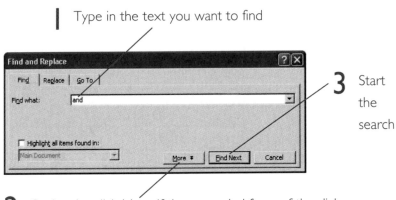

3 Start the search

2 Optional – click More if the expanded form of the dialog isn't visible, then see the DON'T FORGET tip

Replacing text

Word 2002 replaces some words/phrases automatically as you type (e.g. "accross" becomes "across"). This is called AutoCorrect.

To add your own substitutions, pull down the Tools menu and click AutoCorrect. In the Replace field, insert the incorrect word; in the With field, type in the correct version. Click OK.

When you've located text and/or formatting, you can have Word 2002 replace it automatically with the text and/or formatting of your choice.

You can customize find-and-replace operations with the same parameters as a simple Find operation. For example, you can have Word find every occurrence of "information" and replace it with "*information*", or even "*data*"…

Initiating a find-and-replace operation

First pull down the Edit menu and click Replace. In the Find and Replace dialog, click More. Now follow steps 1 and 2 below. Carry out steps 3 and/or 4, as appropriate. Finally, follow either step 5 OR 6:

1 Type in the text you want to find

2 Type in the replacement text

5 Click here to replace the first instance of the specified text

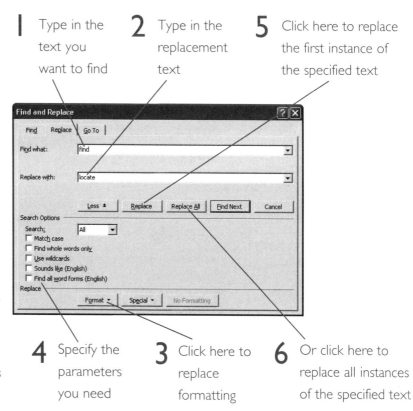

When you follow step 3, Word launches a menu; click the relevant entry. Then complete the dialog which appears in the normal way. Finally, carry out step 5 OR 6, as appropriate.

4 Specify the parameters you need

3 Click here to replace formatting

6 Or click here to replace all instances of the specified text

Searching via the Task Pane

You can use the Search Task Pane to search for files. You do this by entering text; Office then finds files which contain it.

If the Task Pane isn't visible, choose View, Task Pane.

3 Enter text to be found

5 Click Search

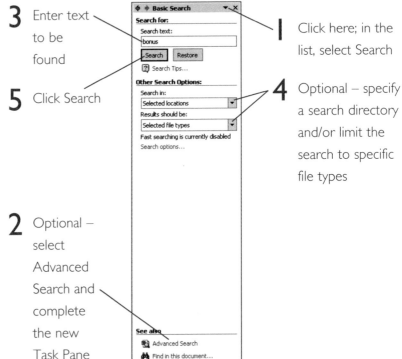

I Click here; in the list, select Search

4 Optional – specify a search directory and/or limit the search to specific file types

You can make the search process a lot faster by using fast searching. Click Install and follow the on-screen instructions.

2 Optional – select Advanced Search and complete the new Task Pane

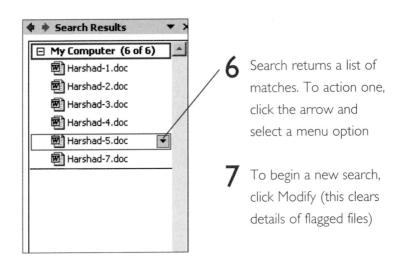

6 Search returns a list of matches. To action one, click the arrow and select a menu option

7 To begin a new search, click Modify (this clears details of flagged files)

Working with headers and footers

You can have Word 2002 print text at the top of each page within a document; this area is called the "header". In the same way, you can have text printed at the base of each page (the "footer"). Headers and footers are printed within the top and bottom page margins, respectively.

When you create a header or footer, Word automatically switches the active document to Print Layout view and displays the Header and Footer toolbar.

Inserting or amending a header

To insert or amend a footer, follow step 1. Now click the following button in the toolbar:

Carry out steps 2–5 as appropriate.

Header/footer text can be formatted in the normal way. For instance, you can apply a new font or type size…

1 Move to the start of your document. Pull down the View menu and click Header and Footer

2 Insert (or amend) the relevant text

5 Click Close to return to normal document editing

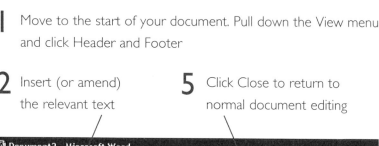

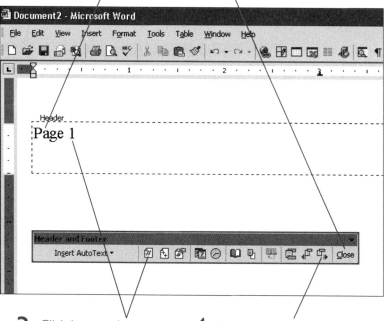

3 Click here to insert a page number

4 Optional – click here to move to the header on the next page

Inserting bookmarks

In computer terms, a bookmark is a marker inserted to enable you to find a given location in a document easily and quickly.

Creating a bookmark

Place the insertion point where you want the bookmark inserted. Pull down the Insert menu and click Bookmark. Now do the following:

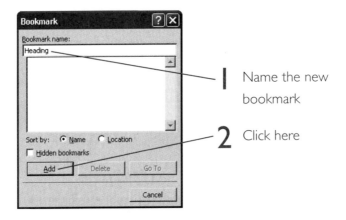

Name the new bookmark

2 Click here

Jumping to a bookmark

Pull down the Insert menu and click Bookmark. Now do the following:

To delete a bookmark, select it then click Delete.

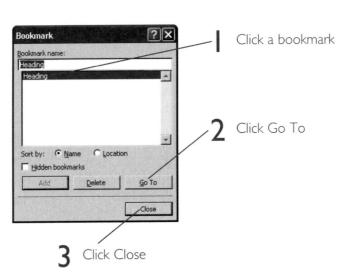

Click a bookmark

2 Click Go To

3 Click Close

Inserting hyperlinks

You can insert hyperlinks into Word documents. Hyperlinks are text or graphics linked to:

To amend a bookmark hyperlink, place the insertion point within it (for text hyperlinks) or select the picture (for picture hyperlinks). Follow steps 1–2. In steps 3–4, make the necessary changes. Finally, carry out step 5.

- another location (e.g. a pre-inserted bookmark) in the same document, or;

- a document on the World Wide Web or an Intranet

Creating a hyperlink to a bookmark

Select the text or graphic you want to be the source of the link. Pull down the Insert menu and do the following:

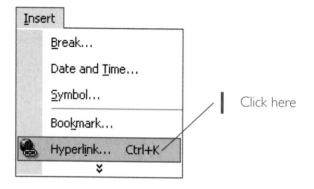

Click here

2 Click here

4 Insert the text you want to display for the hyperlink

To delete a bookmark hyperlink, place the insertion point within it (for text hyperlinks) or select the picture (for picture hyperlinks). Follow steps 1–2. Now click Remove Link.

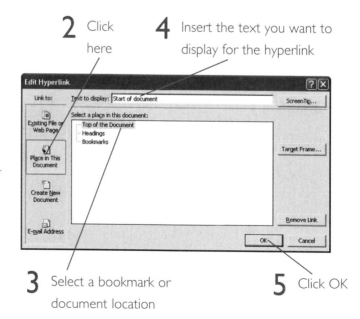

3 Select a bookmark or document location

5 Click OK

To activate a hyperlink, move the mouse pointer over it (but make sure your Internet connection is live if it's a Web link). Hold down Ctrl and click once.

Creating a hyperlink to a Web or Intranet HTML file

1 Select the text or graphic you want to be the source of the link

2 Press Ctrl+K

3 Click here

5 Insert the text you want to display for the hyperlink

To create a hyperlink to a new document, click Create New Document. In the dialog, enter the new document name/address, decide whether you want to edit it now or later and name the hyperlink. Click OK.

4 Type in the Web address

6 Click OK

Creating a hyperlink to an email address

1 Select the text or graphic you want to be the source of the link

2 Press Ctrl+K

3 On the left of the Insert Hyperlink dialog, select E-mail Address

4 Follow step 5 above

5 Enter the address and any subject you want the email to have

6 Click OK

Undo and redo

Word lets you reverse – "undo" – just about any editing operation. If, subsequently, you decide that you do want to proceed with an operation that you've reversed, you can "redo" it.

You can even undo or redo a series of operations in one go.

You can undo and redo actions in the following ways (in descending order of complexity):

- via the keyboard

- from within the Edit menu

- from within the Standard toolbar

Using the keyboard
Simply press Ctrl+Z to undo an action, or Ctrl+Y to reinstate it.

Using the Edit menu
Pull down the Edit menu and click Undo… or Redo… as appropriate (the ellipses denote the precise nature of the action to be reversed or reinstated).

Using the Standard toolbar

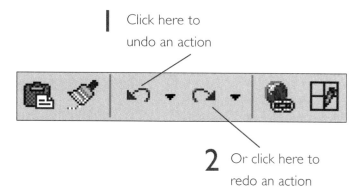

| Click here to undo an action

2 Or click here to redo an action

3 In the list, select 1 or more operations. If you select an early operation in the list (i.e. one near the bottom), all later operations are included

Inspecting text styles

Finding out which text style is in force

If you're in any doubt about which style is associated with text, you can arrange to view style names in a special pane to the left of text.

Pull down the Tools menu and click Options. Do the following:

I Activate the View tab

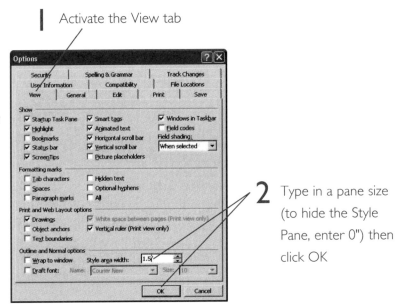

2 Type in a pane size (to hide the Style Pane, enter 0") then click OK

3 To view the Style pane, pull down the View menu and click Normal

4 The Style Pane in action

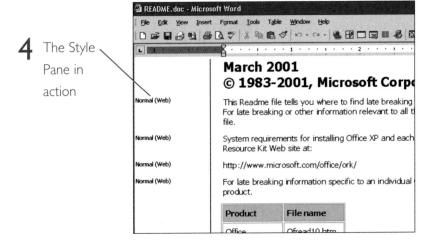

Creating a text style

The easiest way to create a style is to:

A.   apply the appropriate formatting enhancements to specific text and then select it

B.   tell Word to save this formatting as a style

First, carry out A. above. Then pull down the Format menu and click Styles and Formatting. Now do the following:

Generally, new documents you create in Word 2002 are based on the NORMAL.DOT template and provide access to a variety of pre-defined styles, including some specialized ones aimed at the Web.

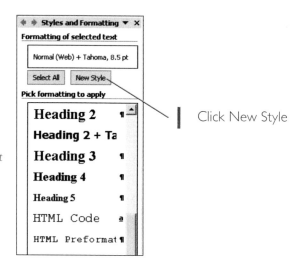

Click New Style

If you want any manual amendments you make to the new style to be automatically incorporated in the style (but only in the active document), check Automatically update.

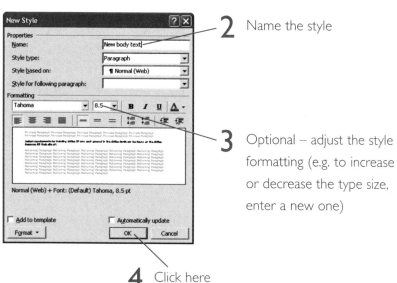

2 Name the style

3 Optional – adjust the style formatting (e.g. to increase or decrease the type size, enter a new one)

Check Add to template if you don't just want your new style to be available for the active document.

4 Click here

Applying a text style

First, select the text you want to apply the style to. Or, if you only want to apply it to a single paragraph, place the insertion point inside it. Pull down the Format menu and click Styles and Formatting. Now do the following:

To delete a user-created style, follow step 1. Right-click a style. In the menu, select Delete. In the message which launches, click Yes.

(When you delete a style, any text associated with it automatically has the Normal style applied to it.)

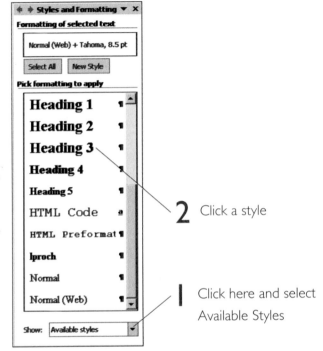

2 Click a style

1 Click here and select Available Styles

Shortcut for applying styles

Word 2002 makes it even easier to apply styles, via the Formatting toolbar.

1 Select the text you want to apply the style to. Refer to the Formatting toolbar then do the following:

2 Click in the Style button; in the list, select a style (entries display with accurate formatting)

Amending a text style

The easiest way to modify an existing style is to:

A.   apply the appropriate formatting enhancements to specific text and then select it

B.   use the Styles and Formatting Task Pane to tell Word 2002 to assign the selected formatting to the associated style

First, carry out A. above. Choose Format, Styles and Formatting then do the following:

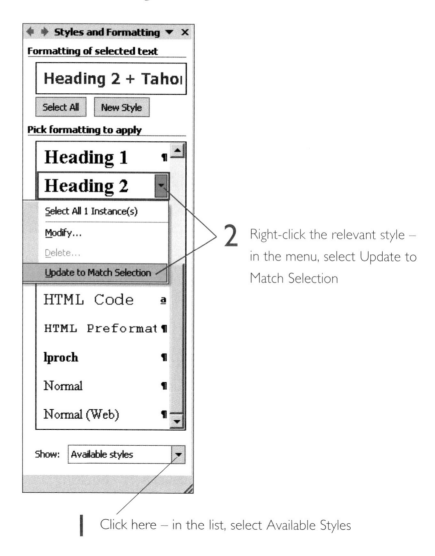

2 Right-click the relevant style – in the menu, select Update to Match Selection

Click here – in the list, select Available Styles

Spell- and grammar-checking

By default, Word 2002 checks spelling and grammar simultaneously.

Word 2002 lets you check text in two ways:

- on-the-fly, as you type in text

- separately, after the text has been entered

Checking text on-the-fly

This is the default. When automatic checking is in force, Word 2002 flags words it doesn't agree with, using a red underline (in the case of misspellings) and a green line (for grammatical errors). If the word or phrase is wrong, right-click in it. Then carry out steps 1, 2 or 3:

Re step 2 – if Word has flagged a spelling error, you have an extra option. Click Add to Dictionary if the flagged word is correct and you want Word to remember it in future spell-checks.

1 Word often provides a list of alternatives. If one is correct, click it; the flagged word is replaced with the correct version

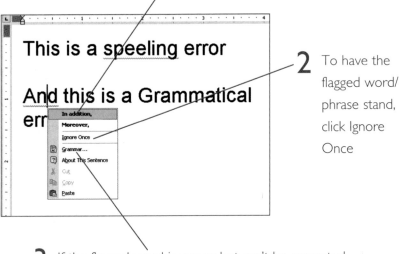

2 To have the flagged word/ phrase stand, click Ignore Once

3 If the flagged word is wrong but can't be corrected now, click Spelling or Grammar and complete the resulting dialog (see the facing page)

Disabling on-the-fly checking

Pull down the Tools menu and click Options. Activate the Spelling & Grammar tab, then deselect Check spelling as you type and/or Check grammar as you type. Click OK.

Checking text separately

To check all the text within the active document in one go, pull down the Tools menu and click Spelling and Grammar. Word 2002 starts spell- and grammar-checking the document from the beginning. When it encounters a word or phrase it doesn't recognize, Word flags it and produces a special dialog (see below). Usually, it provides alternative suggestions; if one of these is correct, you can opt to have it replace the flagged word. You can do this singly (i.e. just this instance is replaced) or globally (where all future instances – within the current checking session – are replaced).

Alternatively, you can have Word ignore *this* instance of the flagged word, ignore *all* future instances of the word or add the word to CUSTOM.DIC (see the tips). After this, Word resumes checking.

Carry out step 1 below, then follow step 2. Alternatively, carry out step 3 or 4.

Word makes use of two separate dictionaries. One – CUSTOM.DIC – is yours. When you click the Add to Dictionary button (see the tip below), the flagged word is stored in CUSTOM.DIC and recognized in future checking sessions.

1 If one of the suggestions here is correct, click it, then follow step 2

If you're correcting a spelling error, you have two further options. Click Add to Dictionary to have the flagged word stored in CUSTOM.DIC (see above). Or Click Change All to have Word substitute its suggestion for all future instances of the flagged word.

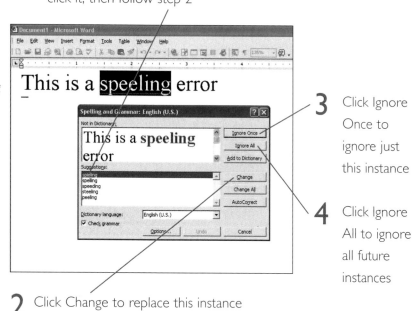

3 Click Ignore Once to ignore just this instance

4 Click Ignore All to ignore all future instances

2 Click Change to replace this instance

Searching for synonyms

Word 2002's Thesaurus may not be installed. If it isn't, follow the on-screen instructions after clicking Language, Thesaurus in the Tools menu.

Word 2002 lets you search for synonyms while you're editing the active document. You do this by calling up Word's resident Thesaurus. The Thesaurus categorizes words into meanings; each meaning is allocated various synonyms from which you can choose.

As a bonus, the Thesaurus also supplies antonyms. For example, if you look up "good" in the Thesaurus (as below), Word lists "poor" as an antonym.

Using the thesaurus

First, select the word for which you require a synonym or antonym (or simply position the insertion point within it). Pull down the Tools menu and click Language, Thesaurus. Now do the following:

1 Click a meaning

2 Click a replacement synonym or antonym

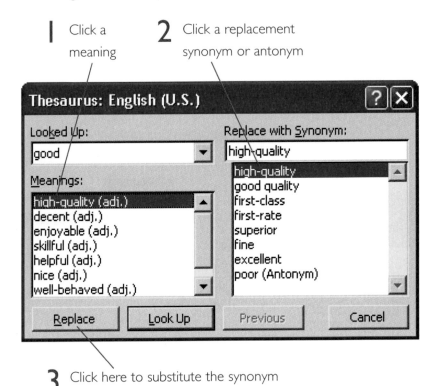

3 Click here to substitute the synonym or antonym for the selected word

Translating text

As long as the relevant dictionary has been installed, you can translate text from within Word.

Translating in Word

| Pull down the Tools menu and select Languages, Translate

2 Enter the text you want to translate (or click Entire document)

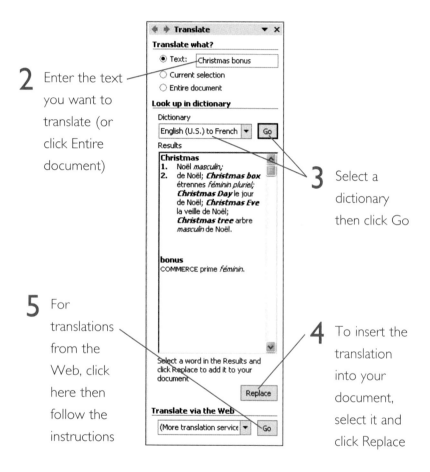

3 Select a dictionary then click Go

5 For translations from the Web, click here then follow the instructions

4 To insert the translation into your document, select it and click Replace

Working with pictures

You can insert pictures automatically, by using Word's AutoCorrect feature.

To set up a picture as an AutoCorrect entry, select it. Pull down the Tools menu and click AutoCorrect. In the Replace field, insert the word/phrase you want the picture to replace. Select Formatted text. Click Add, followed by OK.

To insert a picture stored as an AutoCorrect entry, type in the verbal trigger you set in the HOT TIP above. Now press Space or any other punctuation. Alternatively, press Enter or Return.

Word 2002 lets you add color and grayscale pictures to the active document. Pictures – also called graphics – include:

- drawings produced in other programs

- clip art

- scanned photographs

Pictures are stored in various third-party formats. These formats are organized into two basic types:

Bitmap images

Bitmaps consist of pixels (dots) arranged in such a way that they form a graphic image. Because of the very nature of bitmaps, the question of "resolution" – the sharpness of an image expressed in dpi (dots per inch) – is very important. Bitmaps look best if they're displayed at their correct resolution. Word 2002 can manipulate a wide variety of third-party bitmap graphics formats. These include: PCX, TIF, TGA and GIF.

Vector images

You can also insert vector graphics files into Word 2002 documents. Vector images consist of and are defined by algebraic equations. They're less complex than bitmaps and contain less detail. Vector files can also include bitmap information.

Irrespective of the format type, Word 2002 can incorporate pictures with the help of special "filters". These are special mini-programs whose job it is to translate third-party formats into a form which Word can use.

Compression

You can have Word compress images within documents (making them smaller).

1 In the Picture toolbar, click this button:

2 Complete the Compress Pictures dialog

Brief notes on picture formats

Graphics formats Word 2002 will accept include the following (the column on the left shows the relevant file suffix):

BMP   Windows Bitmap. A popular bitmap format.

CGM   Computer Graphics Metafile. A vector format frequently used in the past, especially as a medium for clip-art transmission. Less often used nowadays.

EPS   Encapsulated PostScript. Perhaps the most widely used PostScript format. PostScript combines vector *and* bitmap data very successfully. Incorporates a low-resolution bitmap "header" for preview purposes.

GIF   Graphics Interchange Format. Developed for the online transmission of graphics data over the Internet. Just about any Windows program – and a lot more besides – will read GIF. Disadvantage: it can't handle more than 256 colors. Compression is supported.

PCD   (Kodak) PhotoCD. Used primarily to store photographs on CD.

PCX   An old stand-by. Originated with PC Paintbrush, a paint program. Used for years to transfer graphics data between Windows applications.

TGA   Targa. A high-end format, and also a bridge with so-called low-end computers (e.g. Amiga and Atari). Often used in PC and Mac paint and ray-tracing programs because of its high-resolution color fidelity.

TIFF   Tagged Image File Format. Suffix: TIF. If anything, even more widely used than PCX, across a whole range of platforms and applications.

WMF   Windows Metafile. A frequently used vector format. Can be used for information exchange between just about all Windows programs.

Inserting pictures

You can use Click and Type to insert pictures in blank page areas.

Inserting pictures via the Insert Clip Art Task Pane

First, position the insertion point at the location within the active document where you want to insert the picture. Pull down the Insert menu and click Picture, Clip Art. Do the following:

1 Enter one or more keywords (these help you find clips)

3 Click Search

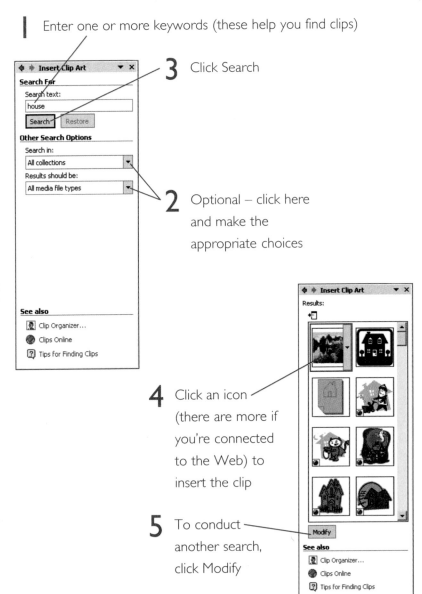

2 Optional – click here and make the appropriate choices

To add new clips to collections (or add new keywords to existing clips), click the Clip Organizer link at the base of the Task Pane.

4 Click an icon (there are more if you're connected to the Web) to insert the clip

5 To conduct another search, click Modify

Inserting pictures – the dialog route

First, position the insertion point at the location within the active document where you want to insert the picture. Pull down the Insert menu and do the following:

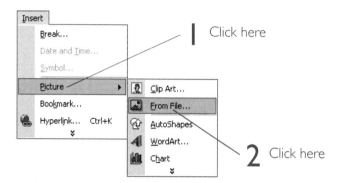

Click here

2 Click here

4 Click here. In the drop-down list, click the drive/folder that hosts the picture

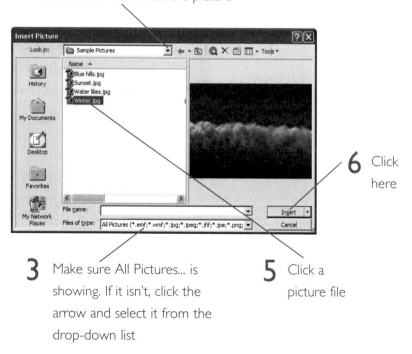

6 Click here

3 Make sure All Pictures... is showing. If it isn't, click the arrow and select it from the drop-down list

5 Click a picture file

Editing pictures

Once you've inserted pictures into a Word 2002 document, you can amend them in a variety of ways. First, you have to select the relevant picture. To do this, simply left-click once on an image. Word surrounds it with eight handles. The illustration below demonstrates these:

Images with the In line with text option active (the default) have handles which are slightly different. They also lack the Rotate handle.

Handles   Rotate handle – drag to rotate

1 To move an picture, just drag it to a new location

2 To rescale it, drag a corner handle to rescale proportionately, or a side handle to warp the image. Drag outwards to increase the size or inwards to reduce it

3 To crop it (i.e. trim its edges so it fits a smaller space, or to remove unwanted parts), click this icon in the Picture toolbar:

Now drag any of the handles inwards

Text wrap

You can control how text wraps around a picture.

1 Select the picture

2 Pull down the Format menu and click Picture

3 Select this tab

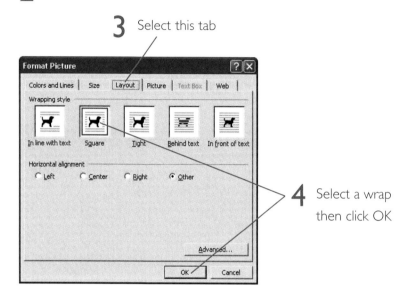

4 Select a wrap then click OK

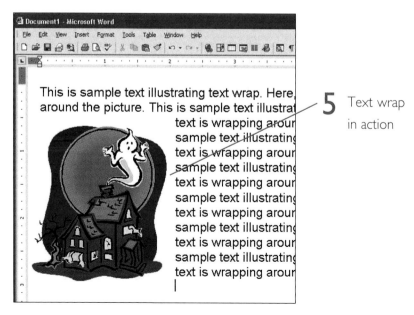

5 Text wrap in action

Inserting watermarks

You can add watermarks (graphics or text printed above or below document text) to Word pages (but not in Web Layout view).

Adding a watermark

1 Pull down the Format menu and click Background, Printed Watermark

2 To insert a picture watermark, check Picture watermark then Select Picture. Use the dialog to find/select a picture. Also, select a scale and – optionally – Washout (makes it much fainter)

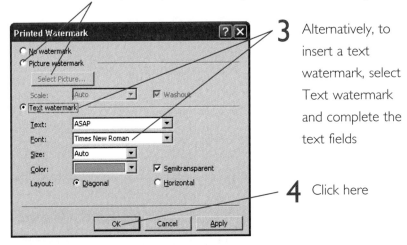

3 Alternatively, to insert a text watermark, select Text watermark and complete the text fields

4 Click here

To amend an existing watermark, follow step 1. Amend the settings in the Printed Watermark dialog then click OK.

To remove a watermark, follow step 1. Check No watermark and click OK.

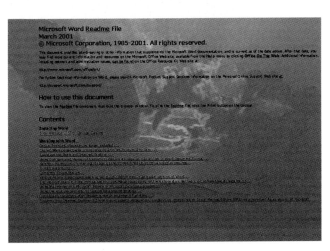

A picture watermark (without Washout)

Inserting backgrounds

In Web Layout view, you can insert backgrounds. These are designed to enhance Web viewing (when you export the file to HTML) but don't print.

Adding a background

1 Pull down the Format menu and click Background, Fill Effects

2 Select a tab then complete the dialog. For example, to add a gradient fill, select the Gradient tab then choose how many colors you want to use, select the colors, specify the brightness/transparency and select a shading style...

3 Click OK

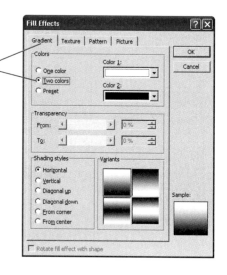

The Gold gradient preset

Bordering pictures

By default, Word 2002 does not apply a border to inserted bitmaps.
However, you can apply a wide selection of borders if you want.
You can specify:

* the style and/or thickness of the border

* the border color

* whether the border is dashed

Bordering clip art
is different.
Double-click the
clip. In the dialog,
select the Colors
and Lines tab and complete the
Line section.

Applying a border

First, select the picture you want to border. Then pull down the
Format menu and click Borders and Shading. Now carry out step 1
below. Perform 2–5, as appropriate. Finally, carry out step 6:

1 | Ensure the Borders tab is active

To set the
distance from the
border to the
enclosed text,
click Options.
Insert the relevant distances and
click OK. Then follow step 6.

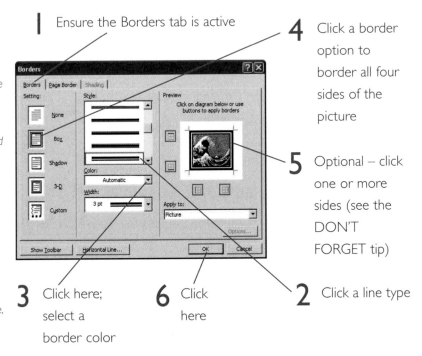

4 Click a border
option to
border all four
sides of the
picture

5 Optional – click
one or more
sides (see the
DON'T
FORGET tip)

Use step 5 to
deselect the top,
bottom, left or
right paragraph
borders. If you
want to deselect more than one,
repeat step 5 as often as
necessary.

3 Click here;
select a
border color

6 Click
here

2 Click a line type

Page setup – an overview

You can control page layout to a great extent in Word 2002. You can specify:

- the top, bottom, left and/or right page margins

- the distance between the top page edge and the top edge of the header

- the distance between the bottom page edge and bottom edge of the footer

The illustration below shows these page components:

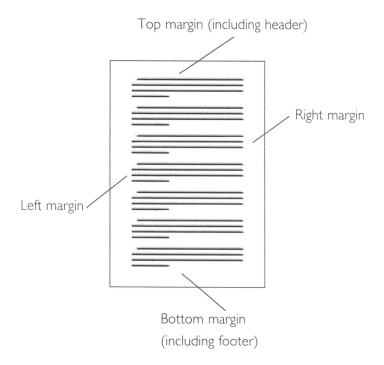

Top margin (including header)

Right margin

Left margin

Bottom margin
(including footer)

You can also specify:

- the page size (irrespective of margins and headers/footers)

- the page orientation ("landscape" or "portrait")

If none of the supplied page sizes is suitable, you can customize your own.

Specifying margins

Margin settings are the framework on which indents and tabs are based.

All documents have margins, because printing on the whole of a sheet is both unsightly and – in the case of many printers, since the mechanism has to grip the page – impossible. Documents need a certain amount of "white space" (the unprinted portion of the page) to balance the areas which contain text and graphics. Without this, they can't be visually effective. As a result, it's important to set margins correctly.

Customizing margins

First, position the insertion point at the location within the active document from which you want the new margin(s) to apply. Alternatively, select the relevant portion of your document. Then pull down the File menu and click Page Setup. Now carry out step 1 below. Then follow steps 2–3. Finally, carry out step 4.

1 Select the Margins tab

2 Type in the margin settings you need

Specify document orientation by clicking Portrait or Landscape under Orientation.

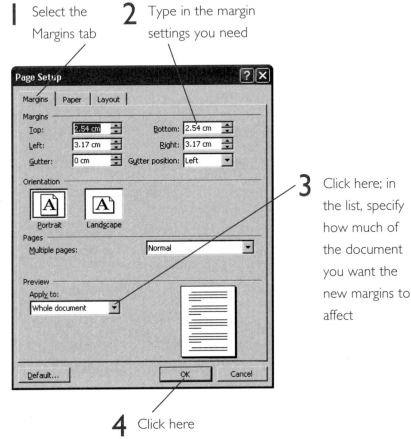

3 Click here; in the list, specify how much of the document you want the new margins to affect

4 Click here

Specifying the page size

Whatever the page size, you can have both portrait and landscape pages in the same document.

(For how to specify page orientation, see the DON'T FORGET tip on the facing page.)

Word 2002 comes with some 17 preset page sizes – for instance, Letter, Legal and A5. These are suitable for most purposes. However, you can also set up your own page definition.

There are two aspects to every page size: a vertical measurement, and a horizontal measurement. These can be varied according to orientation. There are two possible orientations:

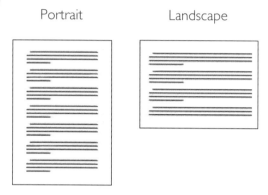

Portrait   Landscape

Setting the page size

First, position the insertion point at the location within the active document from which you want the new page size to apply. Then pull down the File menu and click Page Setup. Now do the following:

Re step 2 – to create your own page size, click Custom size. Then type in the correct measurements in the Width and Height fields.

| Ensure the Paper tab is active

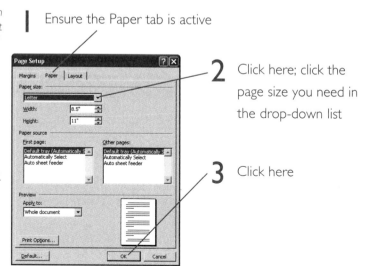

If you don't want your changes to affect the entire document, click the Apply to: field. In the list, select a more appropriate option.

2 Click here; click the page size you need in the drop-down list

3 Click here

Using Print Preview

You can use a special view mode called Print Preview. This displays the active document exactly as it will look when printed. Use Print Preview as a final check just before printing.

You can customize the way Print Preview displays your document in various ways. For example, you can zoom in or out on the active page, specify how many pages display or hide almost everything on screen apart from the document.

Launching Print Preview
Pull down the File menu and click Print Preview:

Print Preview toolbar

You can hide all screen components apart from the Print Preview and the Full Screen toolbars. Click this button in the Print Preview toolbar:

To leave Full Screen view, press Esc.

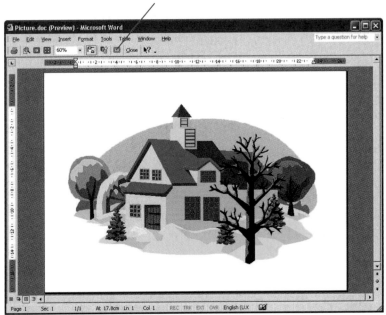

| To edit text directly from within Print Preview, zoom in on the text. Click this button in the Print Preview toolbar:

Now click in the text and make the necessary changes

2 Press Esc to leave Print Preview

Zooming in or out in Print Preview

There are two ways in which you can change the display magnification in Print Preview mode.

Using the mouse

By default, the cursor in Print Preview is a magnifying glass. You can use this to magnify *part* of the document.

If the cursor currently isn't a magnifying glass, do the following in the Print Preview toolbar:

In Print Preview mode, you can view as many as thirty-two (4 x 8) pages at the same time.
Click this button:

In the list, drag until you reach the correct view.

Click here

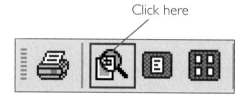

Now position the Magnifier cursor over the portion of the active document that you want to expand. Left-click once.

Using the Zoom Control button

To choose from pre-defined Zoom sizes, do the following:

Click here

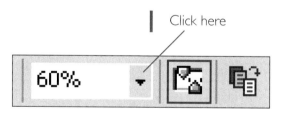

Using the Zoom Control button affects the whole of the active document.

2 Click a new Zoom option (to apply it to the whole document)

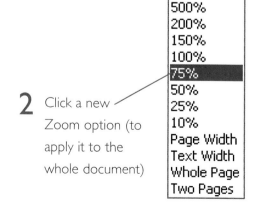

500%
200%
150%
100%
75%
50%
25%
10%
Page Width
Text Width
Whole Page
Two Pages

Printer setup

Most Word 2002 documents need to be printed eventually. Before you can begin printing, however, you need to ensure that:

The question of which printer you select affects how the document displays in Print Preview mode.

- the correct printer is selected (if you have more than one installed)

- the correct printer settings are in force

Word 2002 calls these collectively the "printer setup".

Irrespective of the printer selected, the settings vary in accordance with the job in hand. For example, most printer drivers (the software which "drives" the printer) allow you to specify whether or not you want pictures printed. Additionally, they often allow you to specify the resolution or print quality of the output...

Selecting the printer and/or settings

At any time before you're ready to print a document, pull down the File menu and click Print. Now do the following:

Click here; select the printer you want from the list

This procedure can also be followed from within Print Preview mode.

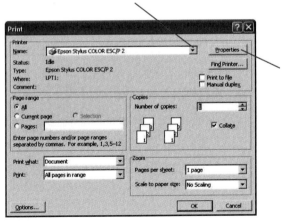

2 Click here to adjust printer settings (see your printer's manual for how to do this)

3 Complete the remainder of the Print dialog, prior to printing your document

Printing – an overview

Once the active document is how you want it (and you've customizes the printer setup appropriately), you'll probably need to print it out. Word 2002 makes this process easy and straightforward. It lets you set a variety of options before you do so.

Alternatively, you can simply opt to print your document with the default options in force (Word 2002 provides a "fast track" approach to this).

Available print options include:

You can preview HTML files or documents (in your default Web browser) directly from within Word. Pull down the File menu and click Web Page Preview.

- the number of copies you want printed

- whether you want the copies "collated". This is the process whereby Word 2002 prints one full copy at a time. For instance, if you're printing three copies of a 40-page document, Word prints pages 1–40 of the first document, followed by pages 1–40 of the second and pages 1–40 of the third

- which pages (or page ranges) you want printed

- whether you want to limit the print run to odd or even pages

- whether you want the print run restricted to text you selected before initiating printing

- whether you want the pages printed in reverse order (e.g. from the last page to the first)

- the quality of the eventual output (with many printers, Word 2002 allows you to print with minimal formatting for proofing purposes)

- whether you want to go on working in Word 2002 while the document prints (the default). Word 2002 calls this "background printing"

You can "mix and match" these, as appropriate.

Printing – the fast track approach

Since documents and printing needs vary dramatically, it's often necessary to customize print options before you begin printing. (See pages 93–94 for how to do this).

On the other hand, there are occasions when you'll merely want to print out your work:

- without having to invoke the Print dialog

- with the current settings applying

- with a single mouse click

One reason for doing this is proofing. Irrespective of how thoroughly you check documents on-screen, there will always be errors and deficiencies which, with the best will in the world, are difficult or impossible to pick up. By initiating printing with the minimum of delay, you can check your work that much more rapidly...

For this reason, Word 2002 provides a printing method which is quicker and easier to use.

Printing with the current print options

First, ensure your printer is ready and online. Make sure the Standard toolbar is visible. (If it isn't, pull down the View menu and click Toolbars, Standard). Now do the following:

You can also access fast-track printing from within Print Preview. Just click the same icon in the Print Preview toolbar.

| Click here

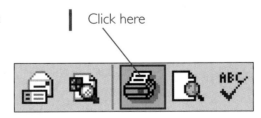

2 Word 2002 starts printing the active document immediately

Customized printing

If you need to set revised print options before printing, do the following.

Pull down the File menu and click Print. Now carry out steps 1–4, as appropriate. Finally, carry out step 5.

1 Click here to deselect collation

2 Type in the number of copies

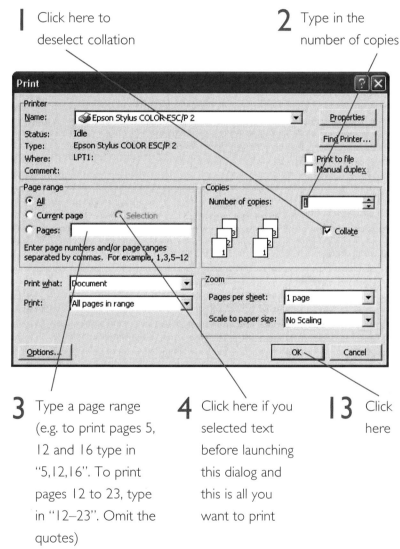

To print only odd or even pages, click the Print field. Click Odd Pages or Even Pages.

To print more than one page on a sheet, click Pages per sheet. Select a number in the list.

3 Type a page range (e.g. to print pages 5, 12 and 16 type in "5,12,16". To print pages 12 to 23, type in "12–23". Omit the quotes)

4 Click here if you selected text before launching this dialog and this is all you want to print

13 Click here

5 For more options, carry out the actions overleaf

Other print options are accessible from within a special dialog. This is launched from within the Print dialog.

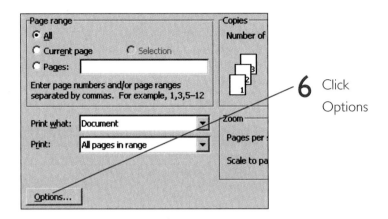

6 Click Options

7 Perform steps 8–12 below, as appropriate

8 Ensure this is selected to print with minimal formatting

If you want to speed up printing, deselect background printing. The drawback, however, is that you won't be able to continue working until printing is complete.

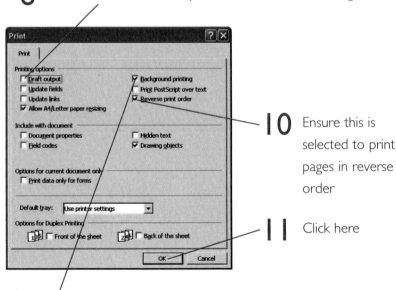

10 Ensure this is selected to print pages in reverse order

11 Click here

9 Deselect this to turn off background printing

12 Follow step 13 on page 93

Excel 2002

Here, you'll become familiar with basic/advanced Excel use. You'll work with data, formulas/functions and error checking. You'll move around through worksheets and use the Watch Window to monitor cells. Then you'll format your worksheets for maximum effect and search for data. You'll use Smart Tags, insert pictures and convert data into charts. Finally, you'll customize worksheet layout, preview your work and print it.

Covers

Chapter Three

The Excel 2002 screen

Below is a detailed illustration of the Excel 2002 screen:

For further coverage of essential Excel 2002 features, see "Excel 2002 in easy steps".

Formula bar   Column letters

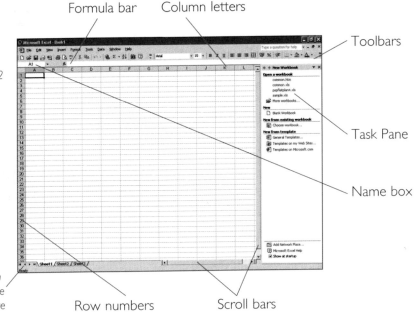

Toolbars

Task Pane

Name box

This is the worksheet Tab area. The screen components here are used to move through Excel documents.

Row numbers   Scroll bars

Some of these screen components can be hidden at will.

Specifying which screen components display

Pull down the Tools menu and click Options. Then:

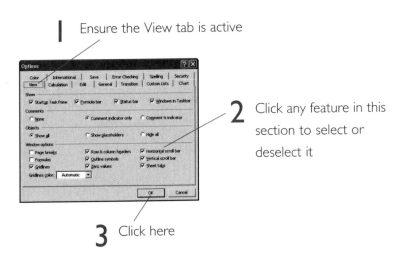

| Ensure the View tab is active

2 Click any feature in this section to select or deselect it

3 Click here

Entering data

When you start Excel 2002, you're presented with a new blank worksheet (spreadsheet):

When you run Excel 2002, you're actually opening a new workbook (see "Beyond cells" below). Excel calls these "Book 1", "Book 2" etc.

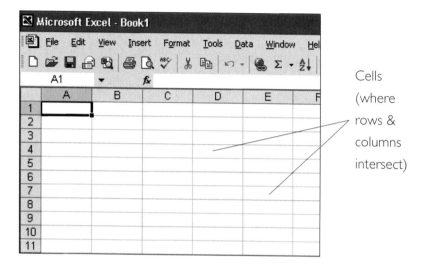

Cells (where rows & columns intersect)

This means that you can start entering data immediately.

In Excel, you can enter the following basic data types:

- values (i.e. numbers)

- text (e.g. headings and explanatory material)

- functions (e.g. Sine or Cosine)

- formulas (combinations of values, text and functions)

You enter data into "cells". Cells are formed where rows and columns intersect.

Columns are vertical, rows horizontal. Each worksheet can have as many as 256 columns and 65,536 rows, making a grand total of 16,777,216 cells.

Beyond cells

Collections of rows/columns and cells are known in Excel as worksheets. Worksheets are organized into workbooks (by default, each workbook has 3 worksheets). Workbooks are the files that are stored on disk when you save your work in Excel.

...cont'd

When you enter values which are too big (physically) to fit in the holding cell, Excel 2002 may insert an error message.

To resolve this, widen the column. Or pull down the Format menu and click Column, Autofit Selection to have Excel automatically increase the column size to match the contents.

Although you can enter data *directly* into a cell (by simply clicking in the cell and typing it in), there's another method you can use which is often easier. Excel provides a special screen component known as the Formula bar.

The illustration below shows the end of a blank worksheet. Some sample text has been inserted into cell IV65536 (note that the Name box tells you which cell is currently active).

Name box

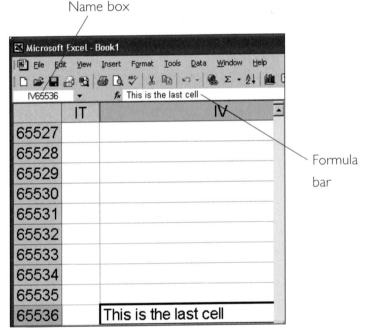

Formula bar

Entering data via the Formula bar

Click the cell you want to insert data into. Then click the Formula bar. Type in the data. Then follow step 1 below. If you decide not to proceed with the operation, follow step 2 instead:

2 Click here (or press Esc)

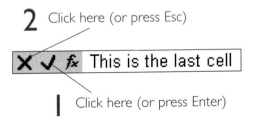

Click here (or press Enter)

Modifying existing data

You can amend the contents of a cell in two ways:

- via the Formula bar

- from within the cell

When you use either of these methods, Excel 2002 enters a special state known as Edit Mode.

Amending existing data using the Formula bar

Click the cell whose contents you want to change. Then click in the Formula bar. Make the appropriate revisions and/or additions. Then press Enter. Excel updates the relevant cell.

Amending existing data internally

Click the cell whose contents you want to change. Press F2. Make the appropriate revisions and/or additions *within the cell*. Then press Enter.

To undo or redo any editing action, press Ctrl+Z or Ctrl+Y.

The illustration below shows a section from a blank workbook:

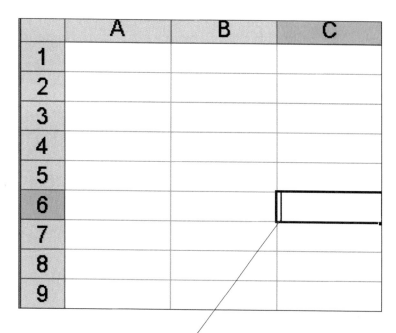

Cell C6 in Edit Mode (note the flashing insertion point)

Working with cell ranges

When you're working with more than one cell, it's often convenient and useful to organize them in "ranges". A range is a rectangular arrangement of cells. In the illustration below, cells A2, A3, A4, A5, A6, B2, B3, B4, B5 and B6 have been selected:

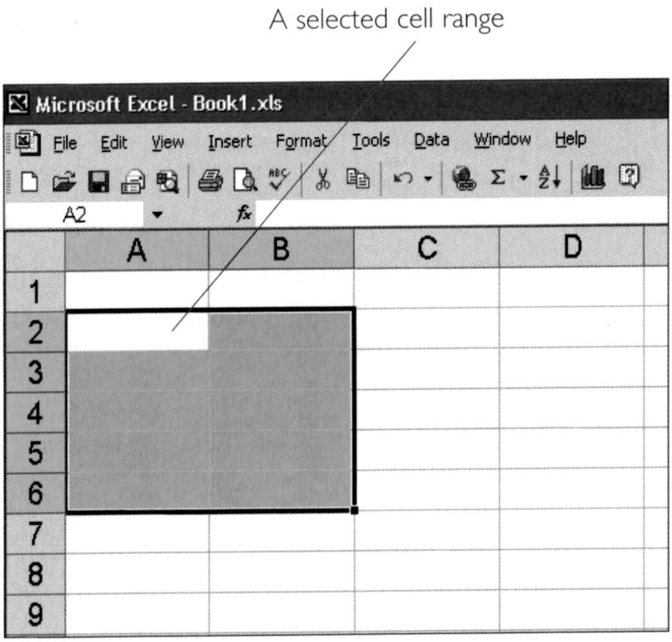

A selected cell range

This description of cells is very cumbersome. It's much more useful to use a form of shorthand. Excel 2002 (using the start and end cells as reference points) refers to these cells as *A2:B6*.

You can extend this even more. Cell addresses can also incorporate a component which refers to the worksheet that contains the range. For example, to denote that the range A2:B6 is in a worksheet called Sheet8, you'd use: *Sheet8!A2:B6*.

Additional shortcuts

You can also use additional reference shortcuts (use the following as guides):

All cells in row 15	*15:15*	All cells in column A	*A:A*
All cells in rows 8–20	*8:20*	All cells in columns P–S	*P:S*

Using Smart Tags

By default, some Smart Tags are disabled (although not the AutoCorrect, Paste, AutoFill and Trace Error functions). To turn them on, choose Tools, AutoCorrect Options. Select the Smart Tags tab and check Label data with smart tags. Click OK.

Excel 2002 recognizes certain types of data and inserts a small purple triangle or blue box in the relevant cell. When you move the mouse pointer over the triangle/box an "action button" appears which provides access to commands which would otherwise have to be accessed from menus/toolbars or other programs.

Two examples are:

The Paste Options button

│ Here, we're pasting in "125" as a new value

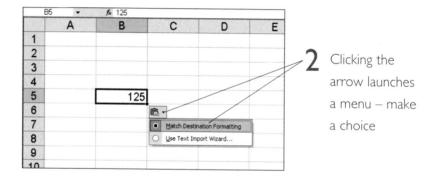

2 Clicking the arrow launches a menu – make a choice

Inserting stock symbols

│ To insert US stock symbols and have Excel provide Web-based information – type MSFT and press Enter

You can search for and download more Smart Tags from the Web. Choose Tools, AutoCorrect Options. Select the Smart Tags tab and check More Smart Tags. Follow the on-screen instructions.

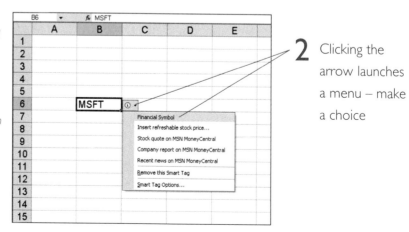

2 Clicking the arrow launches a menu – make a choice

Moving around in worksheets

Excel 2002 facilitates worksheet navigation. As you move the insertion point from cell to cell, the relevant row and column headers are highlighted.

Using the keyboard

1. use the cursor keys to move one cell left, right, up or down

2. hold down Ctrl as you use 1. above; this jumps to the edge of the current section (e.g. if cell B11 is active and you hold down Ctrl as you press the right cursor, Excel jumps to IV11, the last cell in row 11)

3. press Home to jump to the first cell in the active row, or Ctrl+Home to move to A1

4. press Page Up or Page Down to move up or down by one screen

5. press Alt+Page Down to move one screen to the right, or Alt+Page Up to move one screen to the left

Using the scroll bar

1. to scroll quickly to another section of the active worksheet, drag the scroll box along the scroll bar until you reach it (hold down Shift to speed it up)

2. to move one window to the right or left, click to the left or right of the scroll box in the horizontal scroll bar

3. to move one window up or down, click above or below the scroll box in the vertical scroll bar

4. to move up or down by one row, click the arrows in the vertical scroll bar

5. to move left or right by one column, click the arrows in the horizontal scroll bar

Using the Go To dialog

1   Press F5

2   In the Go To dialog, type in a cell reference (its positional identification e.g. H23) or a cell range then click OK

Switching between worksheets

Because workbooks have more than one worksheet, Excel provides two easy and convenient methods for moving between them.

Using the Tab area

You can use the Tab area (at the base of the Excel screen – see page 96) to:

- jump to the first or last sheet

- jump to the next or previous sheet

- jump to a specific sheet

See the illustration below:

When you click a worksheet tab, Excel 2002 emboldens the name and makes the tab background white.

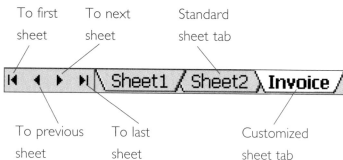

To first sheet   To next sheet   Standard sheet tab

To previous sheet   To last sheet   Customized sheet tab

To move to a specific sheet, simply click the relevant tab.

An example: in the illustration above, to jump to the "Invoice" worksheet, simply click the appropriate tab.

Using the keyboard

You can use keyboard shortcuts here:

Ctrl+Page Up   moves to the previous tab

Ctrl+Page Down   moves to the next tab

Viewing several worksheets

Excel 2002 also lets you view multiple worksheets simultaneously. This can be particularly useful when they have data in common. Viewing multiple worksheets is a two stage process.

1 To open a new window, pull down the Window menu and click New Window

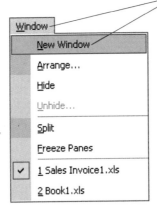

To switch between active windows, pull down the Window menu and click the relevant entry in the list at the bottom.

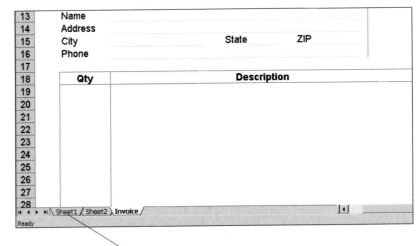

If you want to work with alternative views of the same worksheet – a useful technique in itself – simply omit step 2.

2 Excel now launches a new window showing an alternative view of the active worksheet. Click the relevant sheet tab

Rearranging worksheet windows

When you have multiple worksheet windows open at once, you can have Excel arrange them in specific patterns. This is useful because it makes worksheets more visible and accessible. Options are:

Tiled   Windows are displayed side by side:

Horizontal   Windows are displayed in a tiled column, with horizontal subdivisions:

Vertical   Windows are displayed in a tiled row, with vertical subdivisions:

Cascade   Windows are overlaid (with a slight offset):

Rearranging windows
Pull down the Window menu and click Arrange. Then:

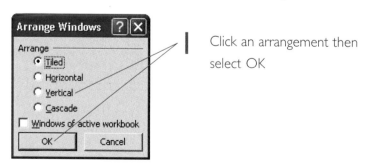

Click an arrangement then select OK

Other operations on worksheets

We said earlier that, by default, each workbook has 3 worksheets. However, you can easily:

- add new worksheets

- delete existing worksheets

- move existing worksheets

To rearrange worksheets, select 1 or more sheet tabs then drag them to a new location in the Tab area.

Inserting a single worksheet

In the worksheet Tab area at the base of the screen, click the tab which represents the sheet in front of which you want the new worksheet inserted. Pull down the Insert menu and click Worksheet.

Alternatively, press Shift+F11.

Inserting more than one worksheet

To add multiple worksheets, hold down one Shift key as you click the required number of sheet tabs (in other words, to add 6 new worksheets, shift-click 6 tabs). Then pull down the Insert menu and click Worksheet.

To move sheets to another workbook, select 1 or more tabs. Pull down the Edit menu and click Move or Copy Sheet. In the To book field, select a host workbook. Then click the sheet in front of which you want the transferred sheet(s) to appear. Check Create a copy if you want to copy rather than a move operation. Click OK.

Deleting worksheets

In the worksheet Tab area, click a single worksheet tab (or shift-click multiple tabs to delete more than one worksheet at a time). Pull down the Edit menu and click Delete Sheet. Excel 2002 launches a special message. Do the following:

| Click here to proceed with the deletion (the worksheet contents are automatically deleted, too)

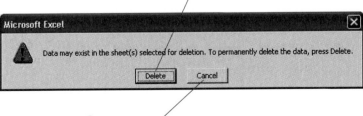

2 Or here to cancel it and return to your workbook

Using the Watch Window

Excel provides a special toolbar called the Watch Window. You can use this to track cells (usually those containing formulas) while you're working on another part of the same or another sheet, or even another workbook. The Watch Window stops you having to continually switch between sheets or workbooks.

Using the Watch Window

| Right-click the cell you want to track

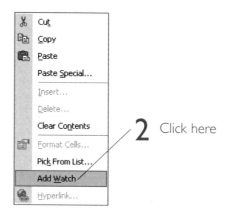

2 Click here

4 To remove a cell from the Watch Window, select its entry and click here

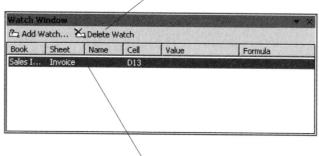

3 The cell has been added to the Watch Window

5 To call up the Watch Window when you don't want to add or remove cells, pull down the Tools menu and click Formula Auditing, Watch Window

Selection techniques

You can also use this technique. Place the cell pointer in the first cell. Press F8 – "EXT" appears in the Status bar. Use the cursor keys to define the selection. Finally, press F8 again.

Before you can carry out any editing operations on cells in Excel 2002, you have to select them first. Selecting a single cell is very easy: you merely click in it. However, Excel provides a variety of selection techniques which you can use to select more than one cell.

Selecting adjacent cell ranges

The easiest way to do this is to use the mouse. Click in the first cell in the range; hold down the left mouse button and drag over the remaining cells. Release the mouse button.

You can use the keyboard, too. Select the first cell in the range. Hold down one Shift key as you use the relevant cursor key to extend the selection. Release the keys when the correct selection has been defined.

To select every cell in a row or column, click the row or column heading. To select multiple rows or columns, click one row or column heading. Drag to select adjacent rows or columns.

Selecting separate cell ranges

Excel lets you select more than one range at a time:

Selected ranges (cells, except the first, are see-through, so you can view changes to underlying data)

To select an entire worksheet, press Ctrl+A.

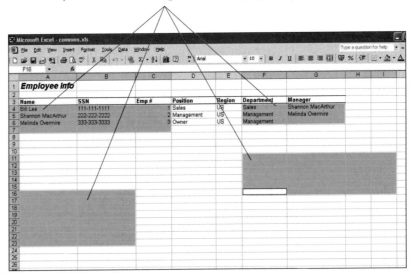

To select joint ranges, select the first in the normal way (you can only use the mouse method here). Then hold down Ctrl as you select subsequent ranges.

Formulas – an overview

Formulas are cell entries which define how other values relate to each other.

As a very simple example, consider the following:

The underlying formula – see below

If Excel detects that you've entered a formula wrongly, it should display a Smart Tag. Click this for help with the formula.

Microsoft Excel - common1.xls

File Edit View Insert Format Tools Data Window Help

B10 ▼ *fx* =SUM(B4:B6)

	A	B
1	**Product/Service Catalog**	
2		
3	**Product/Service Name**	**Price**
4	Fine Lamps	60
5	Leather Chairs	85
6	Hardwood Desks	175
7		
8		
9		
10		320

Total

Here, a cell has been defined which returns the total of cells B4:B6. Obviously, in this instance you could insert the total easily enough yourself because the individual values are so small, and because we're only dealing with a small number of cells. But what happens if the cell values are larger and/or more numerous, or – more to the point – if they're liable to change frequently?

The answer is to insert a formula which carries out the necessary calculation automatically.

If you look at the Formula bar in the illustration, you'll see the formula which does this:

=SUM(B4:B6)

Many Excel formulas are much more complex than this, but the principles remain the same.

Inserting a formula

Arguments (e.g. cell references) relating to functions are always contained in brackets.

All formulas in Excel 2002 begin with an equals sign. This is usually followed by a permutation of the following:

- an operand (cell reference, e.g. B4)

- a function (e.g. the summation function, SUM)

- an arithmetical operator (+, –, / and ★)

- comparison operators (<, >, <=, >= and =)

Excel supports a very wide range of functions organized into numerous categories. For more information on how to insert functions, see page 112.

The mathematical operators are (in the order in which they appear in the list): *plus, minus, divide* and *multiply*.

The comparison operators are (in the order in which they appear in the list): *less than, greater than, less than or equal to, greater than or equal to* and *equals*.

There are two ways to enter formulas:

Entering a formula directly into the cell

To enter the same formula into a cell range, select the range, type the formula and then press Ctrl+Enter.

Click the cell in which you want to insert a formula. Then type = followed by your formula. When you've finished, press Enter.

Entering a formula into the Formula bar

This is usually the most convenient method.

Click the cell in which you want to insert a formula. Then click in the Formula bar. Type = followed by your formula. When you've finished, press Enter or do the following:

Click here

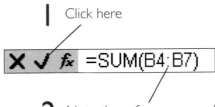

2 Note the references are shown in blue – the relevant worksheet cells should also be outlined in blue

Using the Formula Evaluator

When formulas become complex (as they frequently do), it can be difficult to see how Excel arrives at the eventual result. However, you can now use a feature called Formula Evaluator to step through each calculation.

1 Select the cell which contains the formula. Pull down the Tools menu and click Formula Auditing, Evaluate Formula

3 Each step is shown here – click Close when you've finished

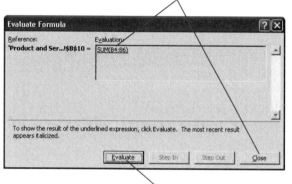

2 Click Evaluate – repeat as often as required

Using the Formula Auditing toolbar

1 Choose View, Toolbars, Formula Auditing Toolbar then:

Check sheet for errors

Show/hide dependents

Launch Formula Evaluator

Precedents are cells referred to by formulas in other cells. Dependents are cells with formulas which refer to other cells.

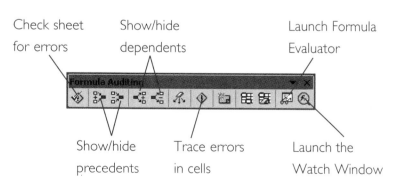

Show/hide precedents

Trace errors in cells

Launch the Watch Window

Inserting a function

Excel 2002 organizes its functions under convenient headings e.g. Financial, Date & Time or Statistical.

Functions are pre-defined tools which accomplish specific tasks. These tasks are often calculations; occasionally, however, they're more generalized (e.g. some functions simply return dates and/or times). In effect, functions replace one or more formulas.

Functions can only be used in formulas.

1 At the relevant juncture while inserting a formula, refer to the Formula bar and click this button: *fx*

2 Type in a brief description of the function you want and click here

If you know the function you want and it's fairly simple, you can enter it directly into a cell (preceded by =). When you do this, Excel often launches a helpful tip.

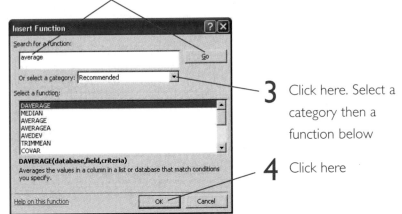

3 Click here. Select a category then a function below

4 Click here

5 Enter the function arguments

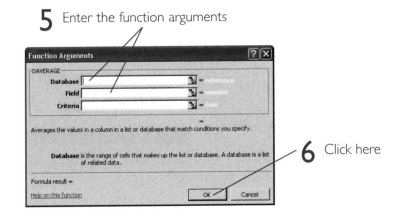

6 Click here

Amending row/column sizes

Sooner or later, you'll find it necessary to resize rows or columns. This necessity arises when there is too much data in cells to display adequately. You can enlarge or shrink single or multiple rows/columns.

Changing row height

To change one row's height, click the row heading. If you want to change multiple rows, hold down Ctrl and click the appropriate extra headings. Then place the mouse pointer (it changes to a cross) just under the row heading(s). Hold down the left mouse button and drag up or down to decrease or increase the row(s) respectively. Release the mouse button to confirm the operation.

Excel has a useful "Best Fit" feature. When the mouse pointer has changed to the form shown in the illustration, double-click to have the row(s) or column(s) adjust themselves automatically to their contents.

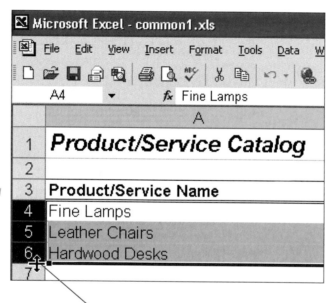

The transformed pointer. Rows 4–6 are being amended

Changing column width

To change one column's width, click the column heading. If you want to change multiple columns, hold down Ctrl and click the appropriate extra headings. Then place the mouse pointer (it changes to a cross) just to the right of the column heading(s). Hold down the left mouse button and drag right or left to widen or narrow the column(s) respectively. Release the mouse button to confirm the operation.

Inserting cells, rows or columns

You can insert additional cells, rows or columns into worksheets.

If you select cells in more than one row or column, Excel 2002 inserts the equivalent number of new rows or columns.

Inserting a new row or column

First, select one or more cells within the row(s) or column(s) where you want to carry out the insert operation. Now pull down the Insert menu and click Rows or Columns, as appropriate. Excel 2002 inserts the new row(s) or column(s) immediately.

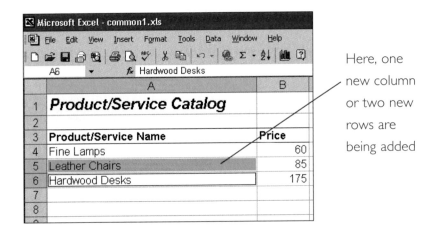

Here, one new column or two new rows are being added

Inserting a new cell range

Select the range where you want to insert the new cells. Pull down the Insert menu and click Cells. Now carry out step 1 or step 2 below. Finally, follow step 3.

| Click here to have Excel make room for the new cells by moving the selected range *to the right*

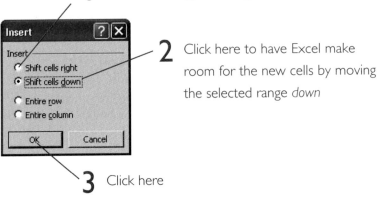

2 Click here to have Excel make room for the new cells by moving the selected range *down*

3 Click here

AutoFill

Excel 2002 lets you insert data series automatically. This is a very useful and timesaving feature. Look at the illustration below:

Types of series you can use AutoFill to complete include the following:

- *1st Period, 2nd Period, 3rd Period etc.*
- *Mon, Tue, Wed etc.*
- *Quarter 1, Quarter 2, Quarter 3 etc.*
- *Week1, Week2, Week3 etc.*

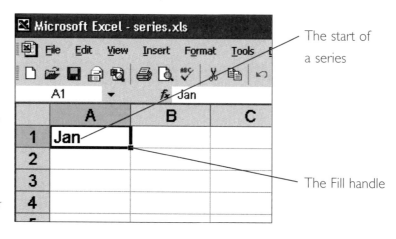

The start of a series

The Fill handle

If you wanted to insert month names in successive cells in column A, you could do so manually. But there's a much easier way. You can use Excel's AutoFill feature.

Data series don't need to contain every possibility. For instance, you could have: "Mon, Thu, Sun, Wed" etc.

Using AutoFill to create a series

Type in the first element(s) of the series in consecutive cells. Select all the cells. Then position the mouse pointer over the Fill handle in the bottom right-hand corner of the last cell (the pointer changes to a crosshair). Drag the handle over the cells into which you want to extend the series (in the example above, over A2:A12). When you release the mouse button, Excel 2002 extrapolates the initial entry or entries into the appropriate series:

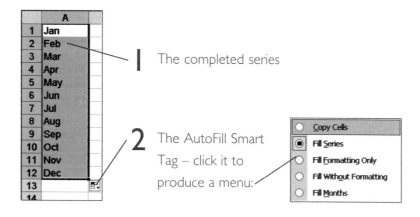

| The completed series

2 The AutoFill Smart Tag – click it to produce a menu:

Changing number formats

Excel 2002 lets you insert and work with Euros. To insert the Euro symbol, hold down Alt and press 0128 on the Numerical keypad. Finally, release the Alt key.

Fonts which support Euros include: Courier, Tahoma, Times and Arial.

Excel 2002 lets you apply formatting enhancements to cells and their contents. You can:

- specify a number format

- customize the font, type size and style of contents

- specify cell alignment

- border and/or shade cells

Specifying a number format

You can customize the way cell contents (e.g. numbers and dates/times) display in Excel. For example, you can specify at what point numbers are rounded up. Available formats are organized under several general categories. These include: Number, Accounting and Fraction.

Select the cells whose contents you want to customize. Pull down the Format menu and click Cells. Now do the following:

1 Ensure the Number tab is active

If a cell has had the Date number format applied, dates appear by default in a specific format. For example, "August 12, 2003" is shown as: 8/12/2003.

To change this, specify a new format in step 3.

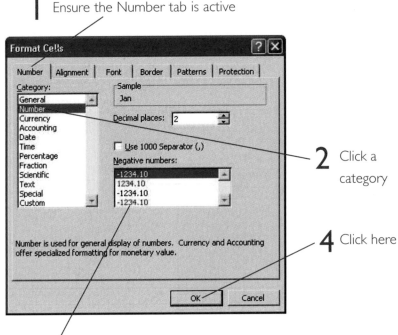

2 Click a category

4 Click here

3 Complete these options (they vary with the category)

Changing fonts and styles

Excel lets you carry out the following actions on cell contents (numbers and/or text). You can:

- apply a new font and/or type size

- apply a font style (for most fonts, you can choose from: Regular, Italic, Bold or Bold Italic)

- apply a color

- apply a special effect: underlining, ~~strikethrough~~, superscript or subscript

Amending the appearance of cell contents

Select the cell(s) whose contents you want to reformat. Pull down the Format menu and click Cells. Carry out step 1 below. Now follow any of steps 2–5, as appropriate, or either or both of the HOT TIPS. Finally, carry out step 6.

To underline the specified contents, click the arrow to the right of the Underline box and select an underlining type.

To apply a special effect, click any of the options in the Effects section.

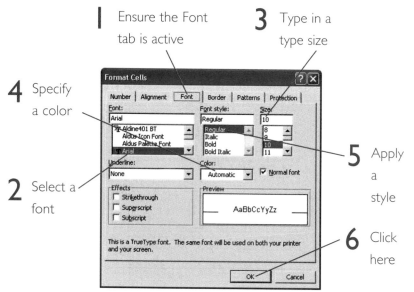

1 Ensure the Font tab is active

3 Type in a type size

4 Specify a color

2 Select a font

5 Apply a style

6 Click here

Cell alignment

By default, Excel aligns text to the left of cells, and numbers to the right. However, you can change this. Alignments come under two basic headings: horizontal and vertical.

Horizontal alignment

General	the default (see above)
Left	the contents are aligned from the left
Center	the contents are centered
Right	the contents are aligned from the right
Fill	the contents are duplicated so that they fill the cell
Justify	a combination of Left and Right

Vertical alignment

Top	cell contents align with the top of the cell(s)
Center	the contents are centered
Bottom	the contents align with the cell bottom
Justify	the contents are aligned along the top and bottom of the cell(s)

There are also alignment aspects you can customize:

Rotation

You can amend rotation (the direction of text flow within cells) by specifying a plus (anticlockwise) or minus (clockwise) angle.

Text wrap

Text wrap forces any surplus text onto separate lines within the host cell (instead of overflowing into adjacent cells to the right).

Text wrap often makes text within worksheets look neater and easier to follow.

...cont'd

To turn on text wrap, select Wrap text in the dialog below.

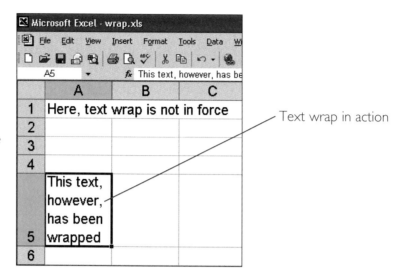

Text wrap in action

Customizing cell alignment

Select the cell(s) whose contents you want to realign. Pull down the Format menu and click Cells. Carry out step 1 below. Follow steps 2–4, as appropriate, then finally step 5.

1 Ensure the Alignment tab is active

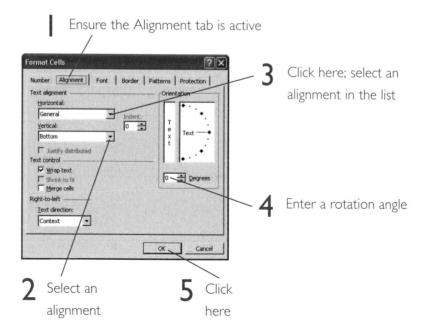

3 Click here; select an alignment in the list

4 Enter a rotation angle

2 Select an alignment

5 Click here

Bordering cells

Excel 2002 lets you define a border around:

- the perimeter of a selected cell range

- specific sides within a cell range

You can customize the border by choosing from a selection of pre-defined border styles. You can also add new line styles to specific sides, or color the border.

Applying a cell border – the dialog route

First, select the cell range you want to border. Pull down the Format menu and click Cells. Now carry out step 1 below. Follow step 2 to apply an overall border. Carry out step 3 if you want to deactivate one or more border sides. Perform step 4 if you want to color the border. Finally, carry out step 5:

1 Ensure the Border tab is active

If you want to customize the border style, apply a line style from the Style section just before step 2.

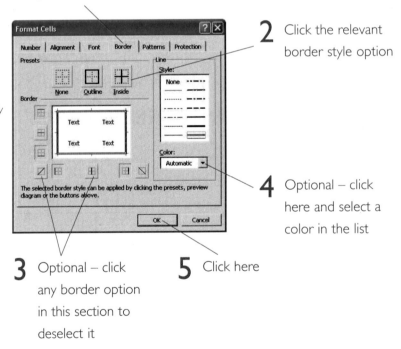

2 Click the relevant border style option

4 Optional – click here and select a color in the list

3 Optional – click any border option in this section to deselect it

5 Click here

Applying a cell border – the Pencil route

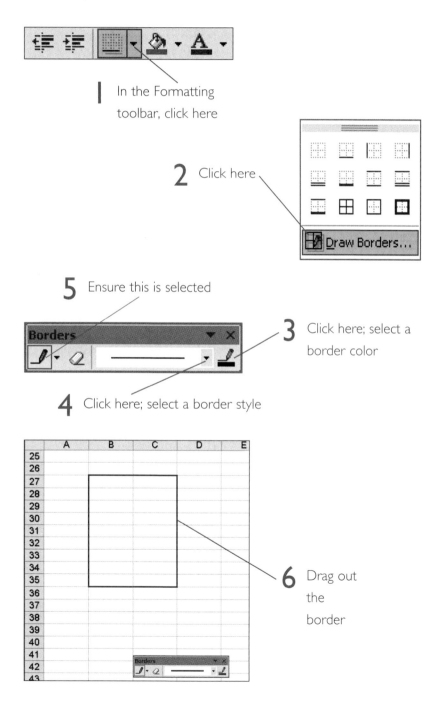

1 In the Formatting toolbar, click here

2 Click here

Draw Borders...

5 Ensure this is selected

3 Click here; select a border color

4 Click here; select a border style

6 Drag out the border

Shading cells

You can only apply a foreground color if you also apply a foreground pattern.

Excel 2002 lets you apply a background color, a foreground pattern or a foreground color to cells.

Interesting effects can be achieved by using pattern and color combinations with colored backgrounds.

Applying a pattern or background

First, select the cell range you want to shade. Pull down the Format menu and click Cells. Now carry out step 1. Perform step 2 to apply a *background* color, and/or 3–5 to apply a *foreground* pattern or a pattern/color combination. Finally, follow step 6.

1 Ensure the Patterns tab is active

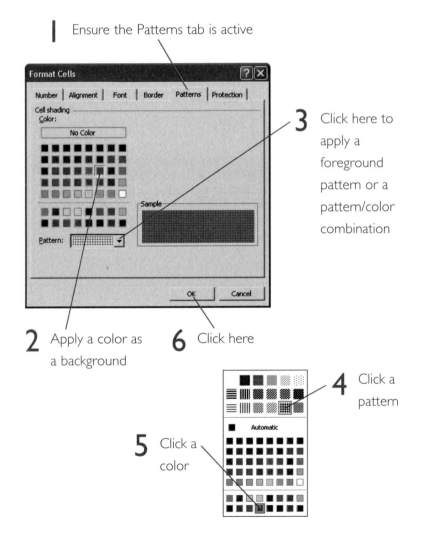

3 Click here to apply a foreground pattern or a pattern/color combination

2 Apply a color as a background

6 Click here

4 Click a pattern

5 Click a color

AutoFormat

Excel 2002 provides a shortcut to the formatting of worksheet data: AutoFormat.

AutoFormat consists of 16 pre-defined formatting schemes. These incorporate specific excerpts from the font, number, alignment, border and shading options discussed earlier. You can apply any of these schemes (and their associated formatting) to selected cell ranges with just a few mouse clicks. You can even specify which scheme elements you *don't* wish to use.

AutoFormat works with most arrangements of worksheet data.

Using AutoFormat

First, select the cell range you want to apply an automatic format to. Pull down the Format menu and click AutoFormat. Now carry out step 1 below. Steps 2–3 are optional. Finally, follow step 4:

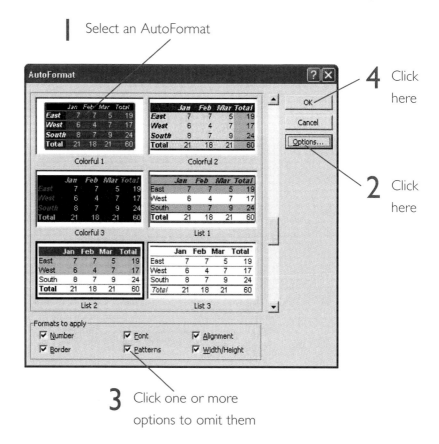

Select an AutoFormat

4 Click here

2 Click here

3 Click one or more options to omit them

The Format Painter

Excel 2002 provides a very useful tool which can save you a lot of time and effort: the Format Painter. You can use the Format Painter to copy the formatting attributes from cells you've previously formatted to other cells, in one operation.

Using the Format Painter

1 Apply the necessary formatting, if you haven't already done so. Then select the formatted cells

Re. step 1 – double-click the Format Painter icon if you want to apply the selected formatting more than once. Then repeat step 3 as often as necessary.

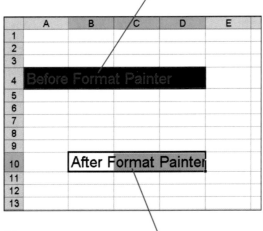

2 Refer to the Formatting toolbar and click this icon:

3 Select the cell(s) you want the formatting copied to

4 The end result

5 Press Esc when you've finished using Format Painter

Find operations

Excel 2002 lets you search for and jump to text or numbers (in short, any information) in your worksheets. This is a particularly useful feature when worksheets become large and complex.

You can organize your search by rows or by columns. You can also specify whether Excel looks in:

- cells that contain formulas

- cells that don't contain formulas

Additionally, you can insist that Excel only flag exact matches (i.e. if you searched for "11", Excel would not find "1111"), and you can also limit text searches to text which has the case you specified (e.g. searching for "PRODUCT LIST" would not find "Product List" or "product list").

To search for data over more than one worksheet, select the relevant sheet tabs before launching the Find dialog.

If you want to restrict the search to specific cells, select a cell range before you launch the Find dialog.

Searching for data

Place the mouse pointer at the location in the active worksheet from which you want the search to begin. Pull down the Edit menu and click Find. Now carry out step 1 below, then (optionally) 2. Finally, carry out step 3.

| Type in the data you want to find

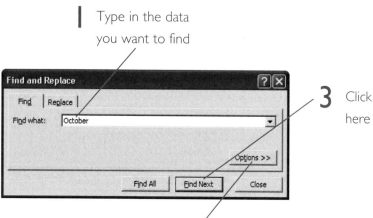

3 Click here

2 To specify the search direction, limit it to certain cell types or make it case-specific, click Options and complete the dialog which appears

Find-and-replace operations

When you search for data, you can also – if you want – have Excel 2002 replace it with something else.

Find-and-replace operations can be organized by rows or columns. However, unlike straight searches, you can't specify whether Excel looks in cells that contain formulas or not. As with straight searches, you can, however, limit find-and-replace operations to exact matches and also (in the case of text) to precise case matches.

Normally, find-and-replace operations only affect the host worksheet. If you want to carry out an operation over multiple worksheets, see the HOT TIP.

Running a find-and-replace operation

To replace data over more than one worksheet, select the relevant sheet tabs before launching the Replace dialog.

Place the mouse pointer at the location in the active worksheet from which you want the search to begin (or select a cell range if you want to restrict the find-and-replace operation to this). Pull down the Edit menu and click Replace. Now carry out steps 1–4 below. Or perform step 5 once for a global substitution.

1 Type in the data you want to find

2 Type in replacement data

3 To set options (see step 2 on the facing page) click here

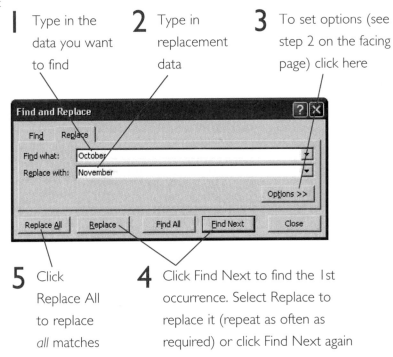

5 Click Replace All to replace *all* matches

4 Click Find Next to find the 1st occurrence. Select Replace to replace it (repeat as often as required) or click Find Next again

Charting – an overview

Excel 2002 has comprehensive charting capabilities. You can have it convert selected data into its visual equivalent. To do this, Excel offers a wide number of chart formats and sub-formats.

You can create a chart:

- as a picture within the parent worksheet

- as a separate chart sheet

Chart sheets have their own tabs in the Tab area; these operate just like worksheet tabs.

Excel uses a special Wizard – the Chart Wizard – to make the process of creating charts as easy and convenient as possible.

A sample 3-D Area chart:

You can add a picture to chart walls. See page 131

Creating a chart

First, select the cells you want converted into a chart. Pull down the Insert menu and click Chart. The first Chart Wizard dialog appears. Do the following:

1 Click a chart type

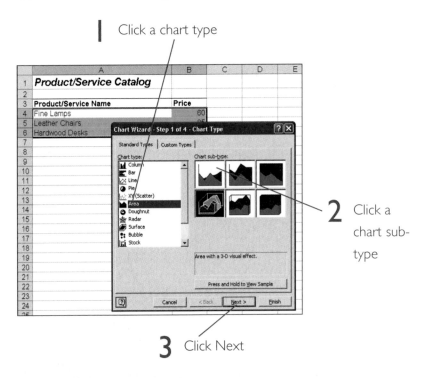

2 Click a chart sub-type

3 Click Next

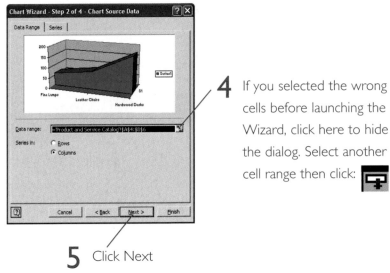

4 If you selected the wrong cells before launching the Wizard, click here to hide the dialog. Select another cell range then click:

5 Click Next

Click any of the additional tabs to set further chart options. For example, activate the Gridlines tab to specify how and where gridlines display...

6 Optional – name the chart and/or axes

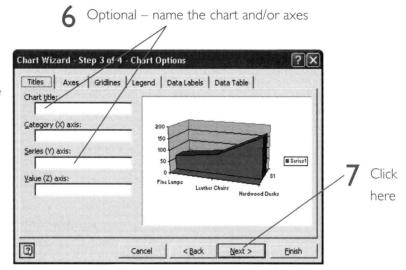

7 Click here

In the final dialog, you tell Excel whether you want the chart inserted into the current worksheet, or into a new chart sheet.

Carry out step 8 OR 9 below. Finally, perform step 10.

8 Click here to create a chart sheet

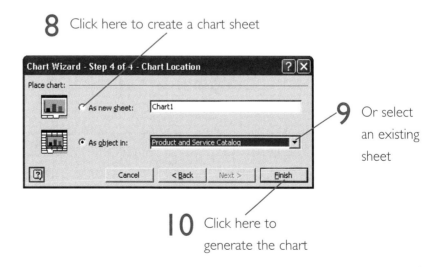

9 Or select an existing sheet

10 Click here to generate the chart

Inserting pictures

Inserting pictures via the Insert Clip Art Task Pane
First, position the insertion point at the location within the active worksheet where you want to insert the picture. Pull down the Insert menu and click Picture, Clip Art. Do the following:

1 Enter one or more keywords (these help you find clips)

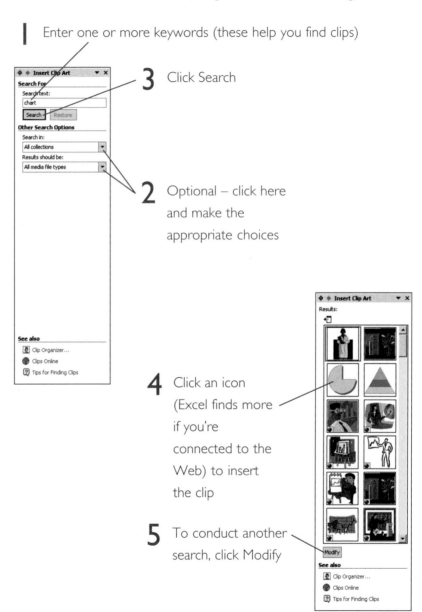

3 Click Search

2 Optional – click here and make the appropriate choices

To add new clips to collections (or add new keywords to existing clips), click the Clip Organizer link at the base of the Task Pane.

4 Click an icon (Excel finds more if you're connected to the Web) to insert the clip

5 To conduct another search, click Modify

Once inserted into a worksheet, pictures can be resized and moved in the normal way.

Inserting pictures – the dialog route

First, position the insertion point at the location within the active worksheet where you want to insert the picture. Pull down the Insert menu and do the following:

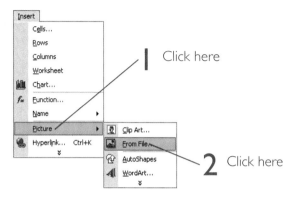

1 Click here

2 Click here

You can insert pictures or clips onto chart walls. First, select the chart wall then follow the procedures described here or on the facing page.

4 Click here. In the drop-down list, click the drive/folder that hosts the picture

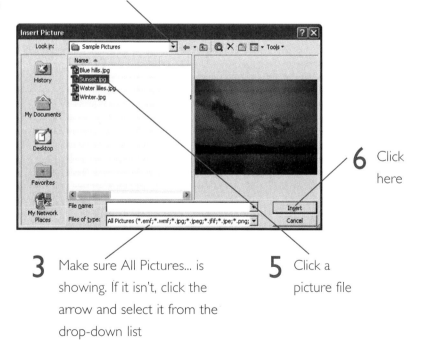

6 Click here

3 Make sure All Pictures... is showing. If it isn't, click the arrow and select it from the drop-down list

5 Click a picture file

Page setup – an overview

Making sure your worksheets print with the correct page setup can be a complex issue for the simple reason that, with the passage of time, most worksheets become so large that they won't fit onto a single page.

You can customize a wide variety of page setup features. These include the paper size and orientation, the scale, the start page number and which worksheet components print.

You can also set the standard margin settings.

Page Break Preview

Excel 2002 has a special view mode – Page Break Preview – which you can use to ensure your worksheet prints correctly.

| Pull down the View menu and click Page Break Preview

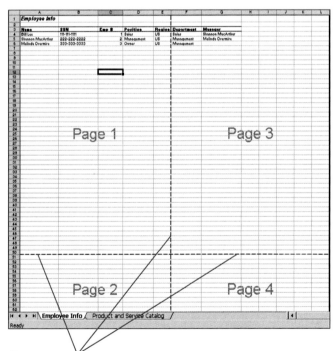

2 Drag page break margins to customize the printable area

3 To leave Page Break Preview, click Normal in the View menu

Setting page options

Excel 2002 comes with 17 pre-defined paper sizes which you can apply to your worksheets, in either portrait (top-to-bottom) or landscape (sideways on) orientation. This is one approach to effective printing. Another is scaling: you can print out your worksheets as they are, or you can have Excel shrink them so that they fit a given paper size (you can even automate this process). Additionally, you can set the print resolution and starting page number.

Using the Page tab in the Page Setup dialog

Pull down the File menu and click Page Setup. Now carry out step 1 below, followed by steps 2–6 as appropriate. Finally, carry out step 7:

| 1 Ensure the Page tab is active | 2 Click the orientation you need | 3 Select a page size |

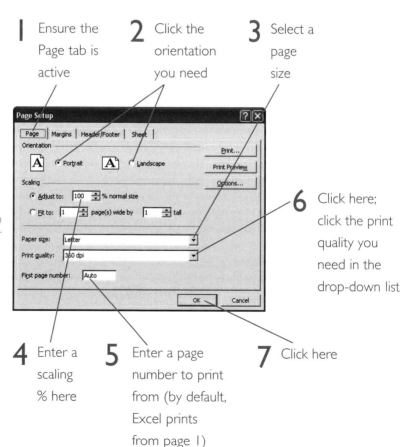

To make your worksheet print in a specific number of pages, complete the "Fit to" fields.

6 Click here; click the print quality you need in the drop-down list

4 Enter a scaling % here

5 Enter a page number to print from (by default, Excel prints from page 1)

7 Click here

Setting margin options

Excel 2002 lets you set a variety of margin settings:

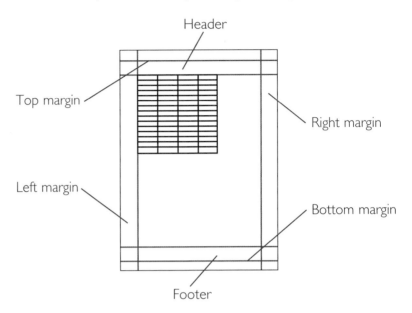

Using the Margins tab in the Page Setup dialog

Pull down the File menu and click Page Setup. Carry out step 1, followed by steps 2–3 as appropriate. Finally, carry out step 4:

1 Ensure the Margins tab is active

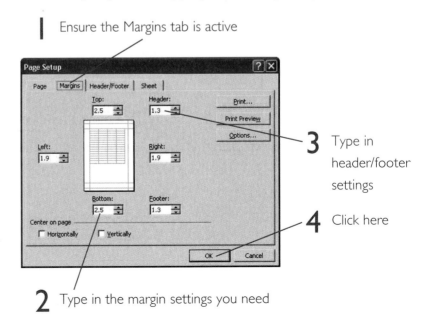

3 Type in header/footer settings

4 Click here

2 Type in the margin settings you need

To specify how your worksheet aligns on the page, click a Center on page option.

Setting header/footer options

Excel 2002 provides a list of built-in header and footer settings. You can apply any of these to the active worksheet. These settings include:

- the worksheet title

- the workbook title

- the page number

- the user's name

- "Confidential"

- the date

Using the Header/Footer tab in the Page Setup dialog

Pull down the File menu and click Page Setup. Now carry out step 1 below, followed by steps 2–3 as appropriate. Finally, carry out step 4:

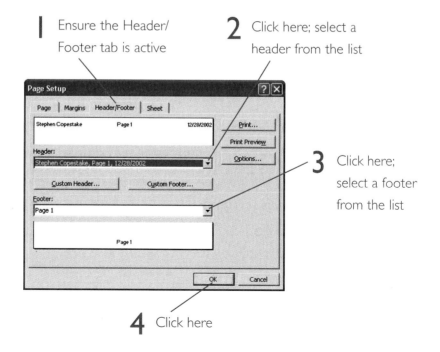

1 Ensure the Header/ Footer tab is active

2 Click here; select a header from the list

3 Click here; select a footer from the list

4 Click here

Setting sheet options

Excel 2002 lets you:

- define a printable area on-screen

- define a column or row title which will print on every page

- specify which worksheet components should print

- print with minimal formatting

- determine the print direction

Using the Sheet tab in the Page Setup dialog
Pull down the File menu and click Page Setup. Now carry out step 1 below, followed by steps 2–4 (and the tips) as appropriate. Finally, carry out step 5.

1 Select the Sheet tab

3 Include or exclude components

If you want to print a specific cell range (print area), type in the address in the Print area field.

Click Draft Quality for rapid printing with the minimum of formatting.

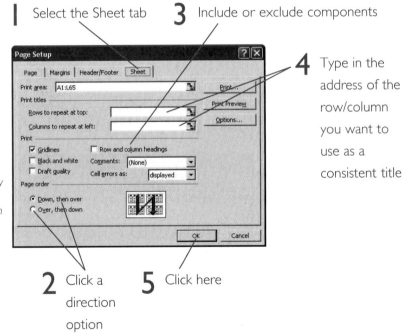

4 Type in the address of the row/column you want to use as a consistent title

2 Click a direction option

5 Click here

Page setup for charts

Most page setup issues for charts in chart sheets are identical to those for worksheet data. The main difference, however, is that the Page Setup dialog has a Chart (rather than a Sheet) tab.

In the Chart tab, you can opt to have the chart:

- printed at full size

- scaled to fit the page

- user-defined

You can also set the print quality.

Using the Chart tab in the Page Setup dialog

Click the relevant chart tab in the worksheet Tab area (or select the chart if it's an object within an existing sheet). Pull down the File menu and click Page Setup. Now carry out step 1 below, followed by steps 2–3 as appropriate. Finally, carry out step 4.

1 Ensure the Chart tab is active

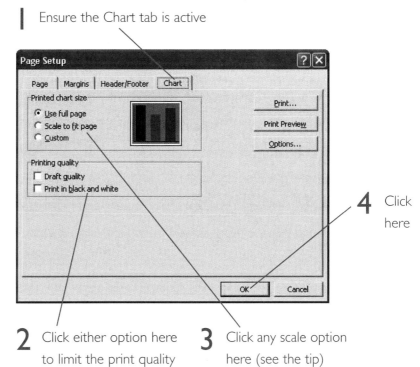

Re step 3 – clicking Custom ensures that, when you return to the chart sheet, the chart size can be adjusted with the mouse in the normal way. The chart then prints at whatever size you set.

4 Click here

2 Click either option here to limit the print quality

3 Click any scale option here (see the tip)

Launching Print Preview

Excel 2002 provides a special view mode called Print Preview. This displays the active worksheet as it will look when printed. Use Print Preview as a final check just before you begin printing.

Within Print Preview, you can move from page to page, zoom in or out, adjust most Page Setup settings or amend margins.

Launching Print Preview

Excel's Print Preview mode only has the following Zoom settings: High-Magnification and Full Page.

| Pull down the File menu and click Print Preview

Special Print Preview toolbar

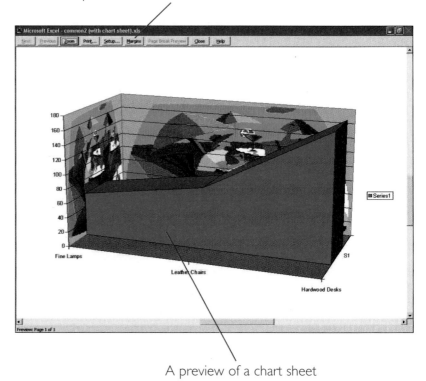

A preview of a chart sheet

2 To leave Print Preview mode and return to your worksheet (or chart sheet), simply press Esc

Working with Print Preview

All of the operations you can perform in Print Preview mode can be accessed via the toolbar.

Using the Print Preview toolbar

Do any of the following, as appropriate:

2 Click here to zoom in or out

5 Click here to launch the Page Setup dialog (see earlier)

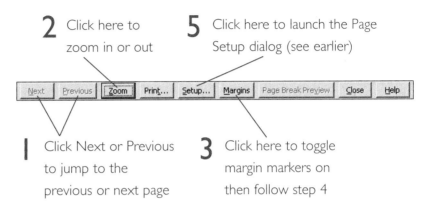

1 Click Next or Previous to jump to the previous or next page

3 Click here to toggle margin markers on then follow step 4

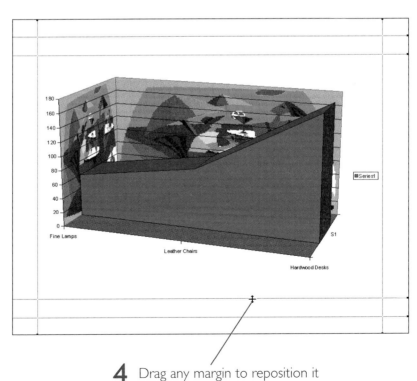

4 Drag any margin to reposition it

Printing worksheet data

Excel 2002 lets you specify:

- the number of copies you want printed

- whether you want the copies "collated". This is the process whereby Excel prints one full copy at a time. For instance, if you're printing three copies of a 10-page worksheet, Excel prints pages 1–10 of the first copy, followed by pages 1–10 of the second and pages 1–10 of the third

- which pages (or page ranges) you want printed

- whether you want the print run restricted to cells you selected before initiating printing

You can print out your work with the current settings applying. This is a useful shortcut for proofing purposes. Just click this icon in the Standard toolbar:

Starting a print run

Open the workbook that contains the data you want to print. If you want to print an entire worksheet, click its tab in the worksheet Tab area. (To print more than one worksheet, hold down Shift as you click on multiple tabs.) If you need to print a specific cell range within a worksheet, select it.

| Press Ctrl+P then perform any of steps 2–6. Finally, carry out step 7 to begin printing

2 Click here; select the printer you want from the list

To adjust your printer's internal settings before you initiate printing, click Properties: Then refer to your printer's manual.

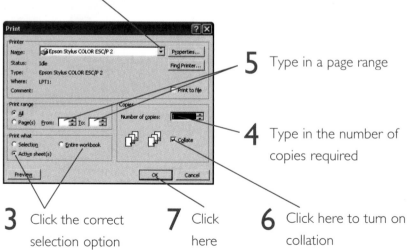

5 Type in a page range

4 Type in the number of copies required

3 Click the correct selection option

7 Click here

6 Click here to turn on collation

Outlook 2002

This chapter explores the stand-alone (i.e. non-workgroup) use of Outlook 2002. You'll use the Outlook bar to launch any of Outlook's associated folders then enter appointments, events, tasks and contact details which Outlook 2002 will now coordinate so that you can manage your business/personal affairs more easily. You'll also use Outlook 2002 to compose, transmit, receive and reply to email, using (optionally) Word 2002 as your editor and working with multiple accounts.

Finally, you'll housekeep your Mailbox, and surf the Internet directly from within Outlook 2002.

Covers

Chapter Four

The Outlook 2002 screen

Below is a detailed illustration of a typical Outlook 2002 screen:

The Folder banner tells you which Outlook folder (in this case, Inbox) is active.

Title bar   Menu bar   Toolbar

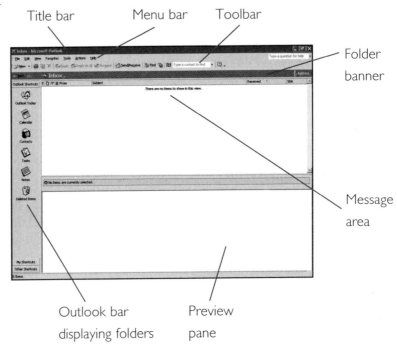

Folder banner

Message area

To print out work you do in any component on the Outlook bar, first click the relevant folder. Press Ctrl+P. Complete the Print dialog as normal. In particular, select a print style – the choices vary with the folder selected. Finally, click OK to begin printing.

Outlook bar displaying folders

Preview pane

There are four available toolbars – you can specify which display.

Specifying which toolbars display
Pull down the View menu and do the following:

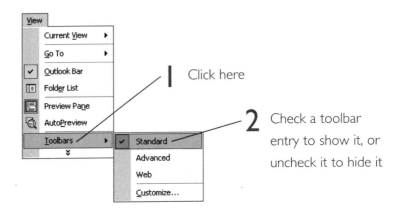

Click here

2 Check a toolbar entry to show it, or uncheck it to hide it

Using the Outlook bar

Outlook 2002 organizes its features into folders. All folders are accessible from the Outlook bar.

When you run Outlook 2002, it automatically opens the Inbox, the folder in which incoming messages are stored. This provides access to often used features. However, there are several additional folders you can access. These include:

Outlook Today	Provides a handy summary of mail, tasks and appointments
Calendar	A tool to help you schedule events, tasks, appointments and meetings
Contacts	A tool to help you manage business/personal contacts
Tasks	A task management aid
Notes	Acts as a pad; you can create "sticky" notes
Outbox	Stores messages waiting to be sent
Deleted Items	Self-explanatory

Activating folders

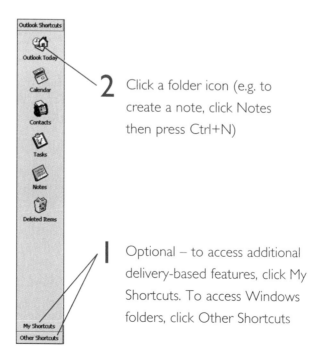

2 Click a folder icon (e.g. to create a note, click Notes then press Ctrl+N)

1 Optional – to access additional delivery-based features, click My Shortcuts. To access Windows folders, click Other Shortcuts

The Calendar – an overview

The Calendar provides alternative ways of viewing and interacting with your schedules. The main views are:

Day/Week/Month

The all-purpose view. An aspect of the Appointment Book; used to enter appointments, events and tasks. You can specify whether you work in the Day, Work Week, Week or Month aspects. (Work Week view stresses the five days of the working week.)

Active Appointments

An aspect of the Appointment Book; used to enter and monitor active appointments

Events

An aspect of the Appointment Book, useful for entering and monitoring events

Some aspects of Outlook 2002 – for instance, the use of the Calendar to coordinate meetings among workgroup members – are beyond the scope of this book.

Switching between the Day, Work Week, Week and Month Calendars

To switch to Events or Active Appointments views, pull down the View menu and click Current View, Events, or Current View, Active Appointments respectively.

You'll probably use Day/Week/Month view more than any other, because it offers great flexibility. By default, this view displays appointments etc. with the use of the Day aspect. To change the aspect, refer to the Standard toolbar and do the following:

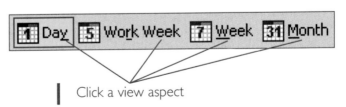

Click a view aspect

Using the Day Calendar

You can add appointments to the Day Calendar. If you want, you can stipulate that the appointment is recurring (i.e. it's automatically entered at an interval you specify).

| To launch Day view, click the Day button in step 1 on page 144

Working with appointments in the Day Calendar
Carry out steps 1, 2 and 3 below (then follow step 4 if you want to mark the appointment as recurring):

An inserted event – see overleaf

2 Select a month/day in the Date Navigator

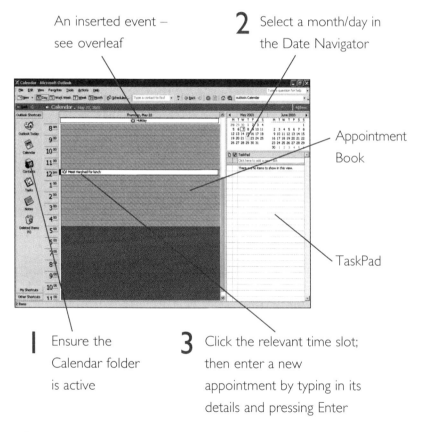

Appointment Book

TaskPad

| Ensure the Calendar folder is active

3 Click the relevant time slot; then enter a new appointment by typing in its details and pressing Enter

4 To edit an appointment, double-click it in the Calendar then complete the dialog. For example, to mark a meeting as recurring, click the Recurrence button in the dialog then set the relevant options

To amend an existing event, double-click its button within the Appointment Book.

You can add events to the Daily Calendar. Outlook 2002 handles events in a rather different way to appointments. For example, they don't occupy specific time slots in your Appointment Book. Instead, they can relate to any day and can even extend over more than one.

Outlook 2002 distinguishes between events and annual events. Annual events occur yearly on a specific date. Examples of events include birthdays/anniversaries, shows and seminars.

Events display as buttons within the Appointment Book (see page 145).

Adding an event to the Day Calendar

Pull down the Actions menu and click New All Day Event. Now do the following:

4 Click here   **2** Enter a description

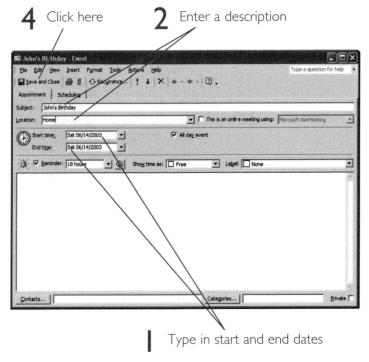

1 Type in start and end dates

3 To mark an event as annual or recurring, click Recurrence in the toolbar. In the dialog, complete any further options. Click OK

Using the Week Calendars

You have to use a slightly different procedure to add appointments. Press Ctrl+N then carry out the procedures on page 150.

Use the Work Week or Week views as an alternative way to display your appointments and events.

In the Week Calendars, you can enter events and appointments. Enter events using the same procedures as for Day view. For appointments, see the HOT TIP.

To launch a Week view, click the Work Week or Week buttons in step 1 on page 144

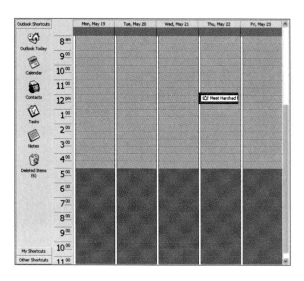

Work Week view – use this to organize your working week

For further coverage of essential Outlook 2002 features, see the companion title "Outlook 2002 in easy steps".

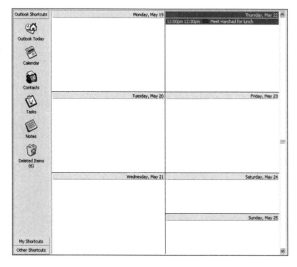

Week view – provides an overview as well as appointment details etc.

Moving around in the Week Calendars

Pull down the View menu and click Go To, Go to Date. Carry out steps 1–3 and 6 to jump to a specific date in the Week Calendars, OR steps 4–6 as an alternative way to switch between views:

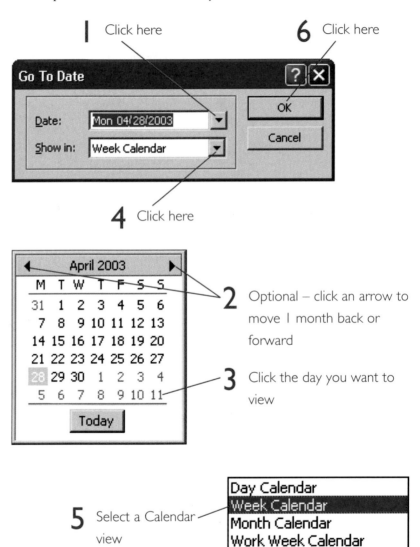

1 Click here

6 Click here

Go To Date

Date: Mon 04/28/2003 ▼

Show in: Week Calendar ▼

OK

Cancel

4 Click here

◄ April 2003 ►

M	T	W	T	F	S	S
31	1	2	3	4	5	6
7	8	9	10	11	12	13
14	15	16	17	18	19	20
21	22	23	24	25	26	27
28	29	30	1	2	3	4
5	6	7	8	9	10	11

Today

2 Optional – click an arrow to move 1 month back or forward

3 Click the day you want to view

Day Calendar
Week Calendar
Month Calendar
Work Week Calendar

5 Select a Calendar view

Using the Month Calendar

1 To launch Month view, click the Month button in step 1 on page 144

2 Use the Month Calendar to gain a useful overview of your schedule:

You can use the Find tool in folders to locate specific data. If the Find tool isn't already displaying at the top of the screen, press Ctrl+E. Enter search data and click Find Now. Any matches are shown below the Find window.

Appointment   Event

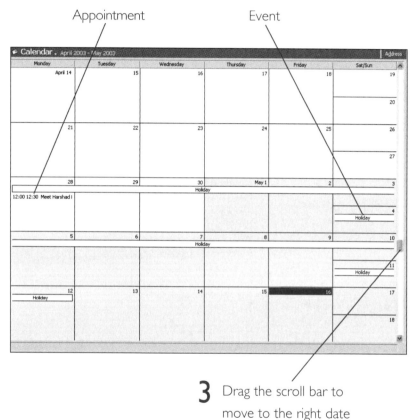

3 Drag the scroll bar to move to the right date

4 Or press Ctrl+G to launch the Go To Date dialog then carry out the appropriate procedures on the facing page

Inserting a new appointment in the Month Calendar

Pull down the Actions menu and click here

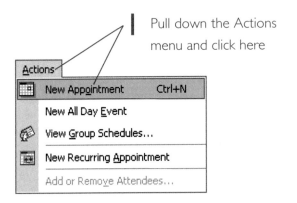

5 Click here **3** Enter a description

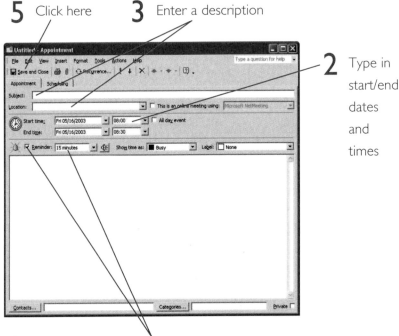

2 Type in start/end dates and times

4 Check Reminder and insert a reminder interval if you want Outlook 2002 to prompt you when an appointment is due

Inserting a new event in the Monthly Calendar

1 Carry out steps 1–4 on page 146

Working with the Tasks folder

Use the Tasks folder to enter and track tasks.

When you've entered a task into the Tasks folder, it displays in the TaskPad in the Daily, Work Week and Week Calendars and in Outlook Today.

If you need to amend or update an existing task, click within it and follow steps 2–3.

Entering a task

1 If the Tasks folder isn't already active, click the Tasks icon in the Outlook bar

Various views are available in the Tasks folder (the view shown here is "Simple List").

To switch between views, click Current View in the View menu; select a view in the sub-menu.

3 Type in a due date, then press Enter

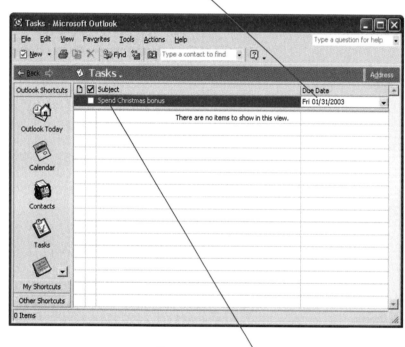

Tasks can be prioritized (Outlook recognizes three levels: Low, Normal and High – Normal is the default).

To set a priority, click the Priority field and select one in the list.

2 Click here; type in a task description

Customizing tasks

The above steps produce a basic task. If you want to customize the settings in more depth (for instance, you can set start and end dates, reminder intervals and/or priority levels – see the DON'T FORGET tip), double-click the task after step 2. Complete the dialog which launches, then click Save and Close.

Working with the Contacts folder

Use the Contacts folder as a convenient place to keep track of business/personal contacts.

To switch between views, click Current View in the View menu; select a view in the sub-menu.

Outlook displays contacts in various forms. The two main aspects are as a grid or using a business card model. Another view (Detailed Address Cards) uses the card model but has more detail. You can enter contacts directly into any view, but you may find that the business card view makes the job easier.

Entering a contact

If the Contacts view isn't already active, click the Contacts icon in the Outlook bar. Then do the following:

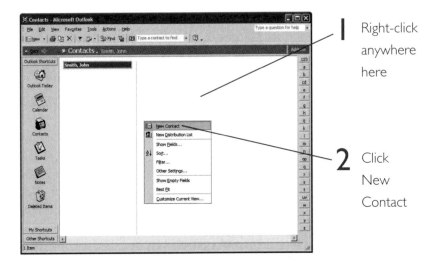

1 Right-click anywhere here

2 Click New Contact

If you need to amend a contact, double-click it. Then carry out steps 3–4 as appropriate.

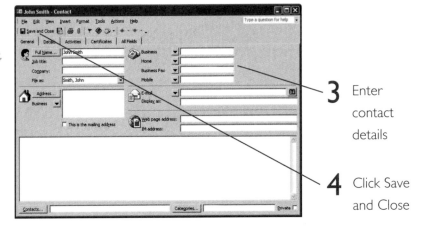

3 Enter contact details

4 Click Save and Close

Composing email

To add a new account after startup, choose Tools, Options. Select the Mail Setup tab and then click E-mail Accounts. Complete the wizard.

(To select an account before sending an email, click the Accounts button in the toolbar.)

When you first launch it, Outlook runs the Outlook 2002 Startup wizard. Among other things, this specifies which email service options you use and sets these up as a new "account". There are two main choices. You can opt to connect via a phone line or by a local area network (LAN). This book assumes you're using the phone-line method exclusively; if you're using the second, consult your system administrator.

After completing the Startup wizard, you should have no difficulty in carrying out the instructions given here and later.

Composing email

If the Inbox isn't currently open, click the Inbox icon in the Outlook bar. Pull down the File menu and click New, Mail Message (or press Ctrl+N). Do the following:

You can use Word 2002 as your email editor. Pull down the Tools menu and click Options. Select the Mail Format tab and check Use Microsoft Word to edit email messages. Click OK. Pressing Ctrl+N now launches a new email in Word.

4 Click Send

1 Type in the email address (addresses are completed from email already sent)

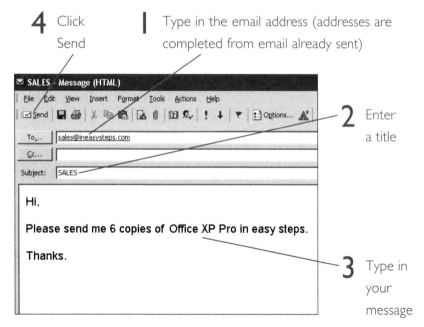

2 Enter a title

3 Type in your message

5 Mail which you've written but which hasn't yet been sent is lodged in the Outbox folder

6 Despatched mail is lodged in the Sent Items folder

Reading and replying to email

Reading email

Once email has been downloaded to you, you can read it in two ways. Do ONE of the following:

To use Outlook as your default email client, follow the procedures in page 40's DON'T FORGET tip.

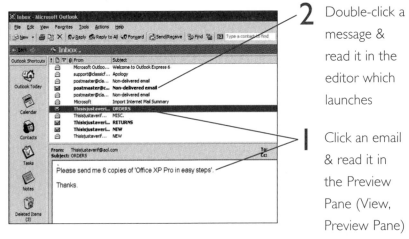

2 Double-click a message & read it in the editor which launches

1 Click an email & read it in the Preview Pane (View, Preview Pane)

Replying to email

1 Click the Reply button in the original message's overhead bar (Outlook uses the format in which the original mail was sent)

Here, Outlook 2002 has launched its own email editor. If you've followed the procedure in the HOT TIP on page 153, Word 2002 will launch instead.

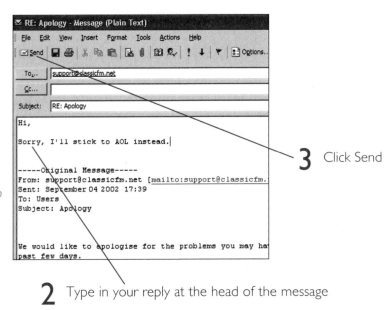

3 Click Send

2 Type in your reply at the head of the message

Sending/receiving email

To send messages or replies you've composed (and simultaneously receive any email waiting for you on your ISP's server), do the following from within any of the email related folders:

Every so often, you should "clean up" your Mailbox. Pull down the Tools menu and select Mailbox Cleanup. Complete the Mailbox Cleanup dialog and click OK.

Click Send/Receive

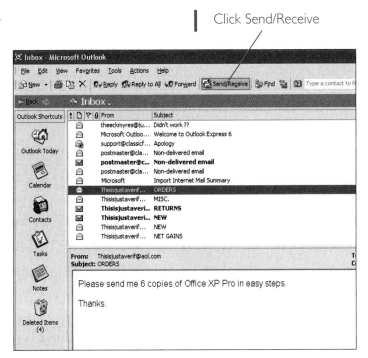

2 Outlook 2002 connects to your ISP, sends your email and downloads any waiting for you. Finally, it closes your connection:

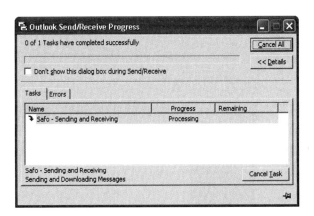

Surfing the Internet

Viewing Web pages directly

First, make sure your Internet connection is live. Refer to the Web toolbar (if isn't visible, click Toolbars, Web in the View menu) and do the following:

Need help with a specific folder? Pull down the Tools menu and click Organize. A special window launches. Click a topic on the left then select and follow an action on the right.

1   Type in a Web address then press Enter

Sending Web pages in email

1   After you've carried out step 1 above, pull down the Actions menu and click Send Web Page by E-Mail

2   Compose your email then click Send

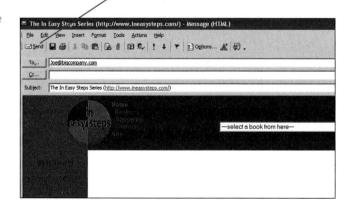

If Word is your email editor, the Web page appears as an attachment instead.

PowerPoint 2002

Here, you'll produce your own professional-quality slide show. You'll automate its creation and then customize it. You'll add/ format text; work with slide views; insert pictures, diagrams, animations and hyperlinks; work with slide masters; and apply new design templates/color schemes. Finally, you'll print out your presentation and run it – in PowerPoint 2002, Internet Explorer and on machines which have neither installed.

Covers

Chapter Five

The PowerPoint 2002 screen

Below is a detailed illustration of the PowerPoint 2002 screen:

Clicking a slide's entry in the Outline/Slide Pane displays it in the Slide area.

Title bar   Menu bar   Rulers

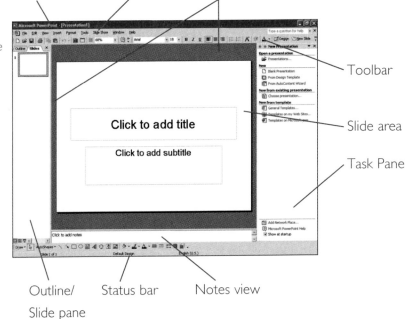

Toolbar

Slide area

Task Pane

You can enter speaker notes into Notes view. Click in it and type in the relevant text. When you've finished, click back in the Slide area.

Outline/
Slide pane   Status bar   Notes view

Some of these components can be hidden, if required.

Specifying which screen components display

Pull down the Tools menu and click Options. Then:

1 Ensure the View tab is active

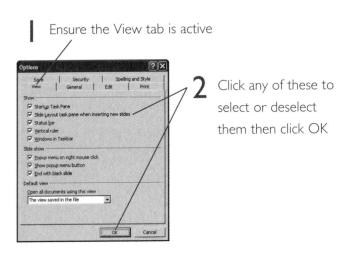

2 Click any of these to select or deselect them then click OK

The AutoContent Wizard

In Chapter 1, we looked at how to create new Office documents based on templates and Wizards. PowerPoint 2002 has a unique and particularly detailed Wizard which handles the basics of creating a presentation.

Creating a new slide show via the AutoContent Wizard

| In the New Presentation Task Pane, click General Templates

2 Ensure this tab is active

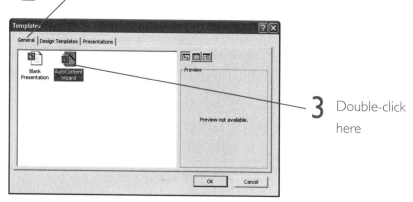

3 Double-click here

The Wizard produces a "standard" slide show which you can amend later, *if you want.*

See Chapter 1 for how to create a blank presentation, or a slide show based on a template.

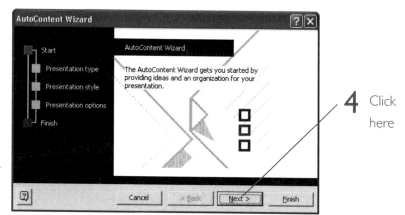

4 Click here

5 Complete the remaining four dialogs in the normal way. In the final one, click Finish to have PowerPoint generate the slide show

The slide views – an overview

PowerPoint's principal views

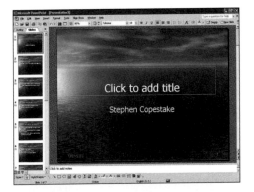

Normal view – displays each slide individually

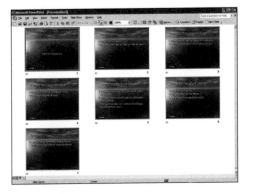

Slide Sorter view – shows all the slides as icons, so you can manipulate them more easily

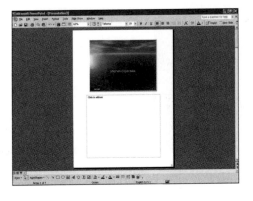

Notes Page view – shows each slide plus any speaker notes

Switching to a view

Pull down the View menu and click the relevant view entry

Normal view also has important subsidiary views.

Secondary views

1 If the Outline/Slide page isn't visible in Normal view, choose View, Normal (Restore Panes)

2 Click the appropriate tab

3 Slide view – shows thumbnails for each slide

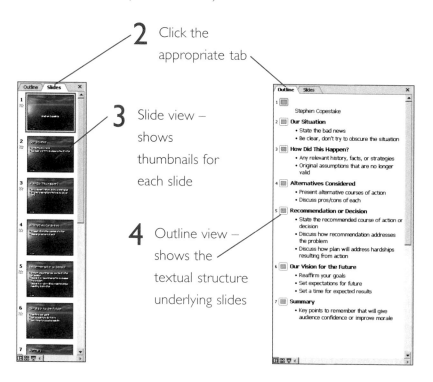

4 Outline view – shows the textual structure underlying slides

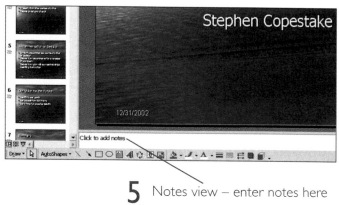

5 Notes view – enter notes here

Using the slide views

All the views have their own default magnification. You can adjust this, however. Pull down the View menu and click Zoom. Select a new percentage and click OK.

The following are some brief supplementary notes on how best to use the PowerPoint 2002 views.

Normal view

Normal view displays the current slide in its own window. Use Normal view when you want a detailed picture of a slide (for instance, when you amend any of the slide contents, or when you change the overall formatting).

You can also use Normal view to:

* work with text. The Outline component of the Outline/Slide pane (see page 158) displays only text. You can amend this and watch your changes take effect in the Slide area on the right

* enter notes. Simply click in the Notes view below the Slide area and enter speaker note text. (You can also do this within Notes Page view – see below)

To switch from slide to slide, you can press Page Up or Page Down as appropriate. (For more information on how to move around in presentations, see "Moving through presentations" on page 172.)

Slide Sorter view

You can also use Slide Sorter view to perform additional operations – for instance, you can use it to apply a new slide layout to more than one slide at a time.

If you need to rearrange the order of slides, use Slide Sorter view. You can simply click on a slide and drag it to a new location (to move more than one slide, hold down one Ctrl key as you click them, then release the key and drag). You can also copy a slide by holding down Ctrl as you drag.

Notes Page view

This view is an aid to the presenter rather than the viewer of the slide show. If you want to enter speaker notes on a slide (for later printing), use Notes Page view.

In Notes Page view, the slide is displayed at a reduced size at the top of the page. Below this is a standard PowerPoint 2002 text object. For how to enter notes in this, see the "Adding text to slides" topic on page 165.

Using grids

You can add a grid to slides within Normal or Notes Page views. This is a useful feature because you can align objects (e.g. pictures) to it.

Enabling the grid

Ensure Snap objects to grid is checked to have objects "attracted" to the grid.

| In Normal or Notes Page view, pull down the View menu and select Grid and Guides

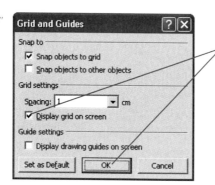

2 Ensure Display grid on screen is checked then confirm

You can also apply manual ("drawing") guides. Ensure Display drawing guides on screen is checked. When you close the dialog 1 horizontal and 1 vertical line appear on-screen; drag these to a new location and align objects with them.

The grid structure

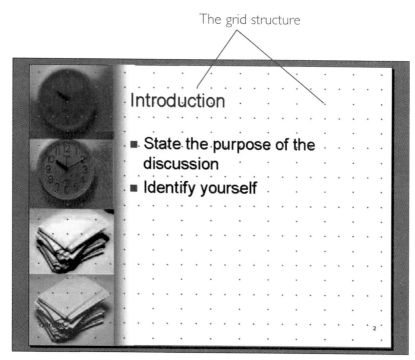

Customizing slide structure

You can select more than one slide in Slide Sorter view by holding down Ctrl as you click on the slide icons.

The easiest way to customize the basic format of a slide is to use preset layouts. There are almost 30 of these under various headings (Text, Content, Text and Content and Other). You can apply layouts to one or more slides. When you've done this, you can then amend the individual components (see later topics).

Using preset layouts

Make sure you're in Normal or Slide Sorter view. If you're in Slide Sorter view, click the slide(s) you want to amend. Pull down the Format menu and click Slide Layout.

You can also use the Slide component of the Outline/Slide pane to select multiple slides. Ctrl+click to select thumbnails.

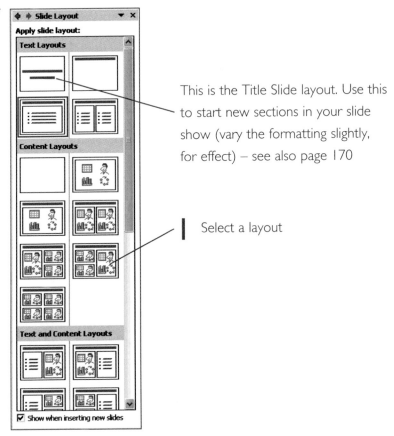

This is the Title Slide layout. Use this to start new sections in your slide show (vary the formatting slightly, for effect) – see also page 170

Select a layout

2 Any slide components present before you applied the new format will still remain. However, they may need to be resized or moved

Adding text to slides

When you create a new slide show, PowerPoint 2002 fills each slide with placeholders containing sample text. The idea is that you should replace this with your own text.

To create a blank slide show (as here), press Ctrl+N.

When you type in text, certain errors are automatically corrected for example:

- *the first letter in sentences is capitalised*
- *day names are capitalised*
- *specific errors are corrected (e.g. "abbout" becomes "about")*

All these generate AutoCorrect Smart Tags. Clicking the blue box under the substitution produces a menu; select the appropriate option.

| Click in a placeholder

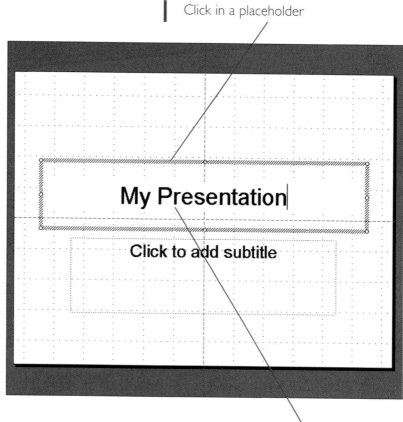

2 PowerPoint displays a text entry box – type in your own text

3 Click anywhere outside the placeholder to confirm the addition of the new text

Formatting text

Font-based formatting

1 Click inside the relevant text object and select the text you want to format

2 Pull down the Format menu and click Font then carry out any of steps 3–8 below, as appropriate. Finally, follow step 9:

3 Select a typeface

4 Type in a new point size

9 Click here

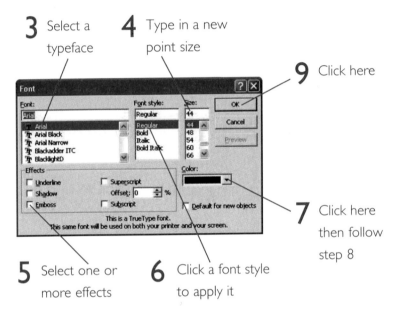

5 Select one or more effects

6 Click a font style to apply it

7 Click here then follow step 8

8 Click a color. If none are suitable, click More Colors and select one in the new dialog

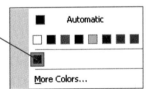

Changing text alignment

1 Click inside the relevant text object and select the text whose alignment you want to amend

2 Pull down the Format menu and click Alignment. In the submenu, select an alignment

Changing text spacing

| Click inside the relevant text object and select the text whose alignment you want to amend

2 Pull down the Format menu and click Line Spacing

3 Type in a line spacing

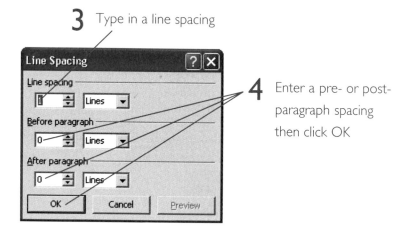

4 Enter a pre- or post-paragraph spacing then click OK

Summarizing slides

You can collect slide titles and insert them into a new slide.

| In Slide Sorter view, select the slides you want to include then click this toolbar button:

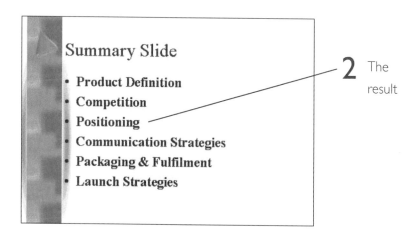

2 The result

Color schemes & design templates

Applying a new color scheme or design template is a quick and effective way to give a presentation a new and consistent look.

Any PowerPoint presentation (apart from a blank one) has various color schemes/design templates available to it.

Imposing a color scheme/design template

1 Pull down the Format menu and click Slide Design

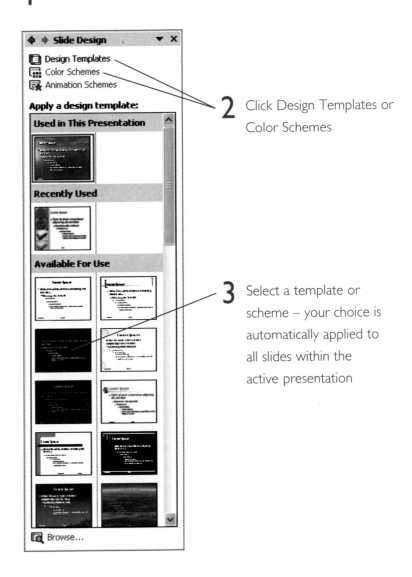

2 Click Design Templates or Color Schemes

3 Select a template or scheme – your choice is automatically applied to all slides within the active presentation

Slide masters

When you apply a design template, PowerPoint automatically adds a "slide master" to your presentation. The idea of slide masters is that you can change or add an element and have this automatically reflected in all the associated slides. Typical uses for slide masters include:

- inserting pictures (e.g. logos) which you want to appear on all slides

- implementing font formatting which you want to appear on all slides

Editing slide masters

PowerPoint 2002 slide shows can have multiple slide masters.

1 | Pull down the View menu and click Master, Slide Master

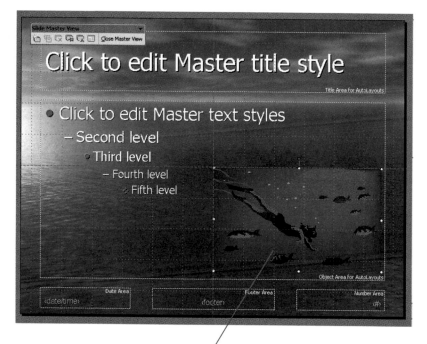

2 Edit the master – e.g. by reformatting text (you can't change the text itself) or (as here) adding pictures

Title masters

Most slide masters are associated with title masters. Use title masters to adjust slides which use a title slide layout (see also page 164).

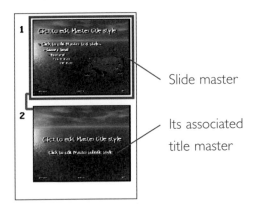

Slide master

Its associated
title master

Handouts often accompany presentations. To customize handouts, choose View, Master, Handout Master. Edit any of the placeholders or customize the background (right-click the background and select Handout Background). Or use the toolbar to specify the number of handouts per page.

Notes masters

You can also customize how notes are presented by using the Notes master.

| Pull down the View menu and click Master, Notes Master

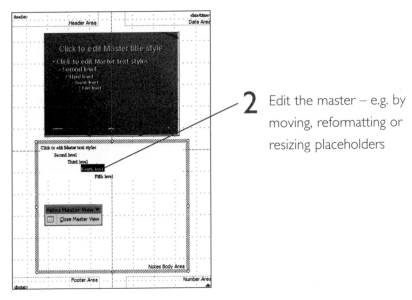

2 Edit the master – e.g. by moving, reformatting or resizing placeholders

Format Painter

You can use Format Painter to copy formatting between text. Format Painter can also copy any formatting you've applied to a picture (e.g. a border) to another image.

PowerPoint 2002 offers a useful shortcut (the Format Painter) which enables you to copy a color scheme from one presentation to one or more slides in another.

Copying color schemes

1. With both presentations open in Normal view, pull down the Window menu and click Arrange All

2. Carry out step 3 below. In step 4, single-click for one copy or double-click for multiple copies (and see the HOT TIP)

To copy the formatting to more than one slide, double-click in step 4. In step 5, click as many icons as required. When you've finished, press Esc.

4. In the Standard toolbar, click or double-click the Format Painter icon:

3. Click the icon for the slide whose scheme you want to copy

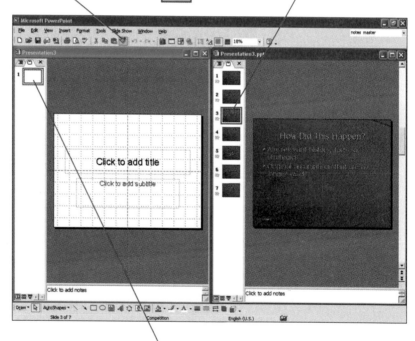

5. Click the icon representing the slide you want to format

Moving through presentations

Since presentations – by their very nature – always have more than one slide, it's essential to be able to move from slide to slide easily (it's even more essential in the case of especially large presentations). There are two main methods you can use to do this.

Using the vertical scroll bar

PowerPoint lets you broadcast slide shows over Intranets. For help with any aspect of slide show broadcasting (inc. scheduling the broadcast via Outlook), see your system administrator.

In Normal or Notes Page views, move the mouse pointer over the vertical scroll box. Hold down the left mouse button and drag the box up or down. As you do so, PowerPoint 2002 displays a message box giving you the number and title of the slide you're up to.

Slide number indicator – when the correct number displays, release the mouse button to jump to that slide

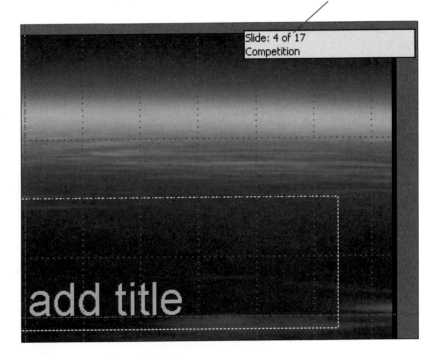

Slide: 4 of 17
Competition

add title

Using Slide Sorter view

Slide Sorter view offers a useful shortcut which you can use to jump immediately to a specific slide. Simply double-click any slide icon within Slide Sorter view; PowerPoint then switches to Slide view and displays the slide you selected.

Inserting and deleting slides

You'll often want to insert a new slide into presentations.

Inserting a slide

1 In Normal or Notes Page view, move to the slide you want to precede the new one. In Slide Sorter view, click the relevant slide

2 Pull down the Insert menu and click New Slide

To delete a slide, pull down the Edit menu and click Delete Slide (the slide and its contents are erased immediately).

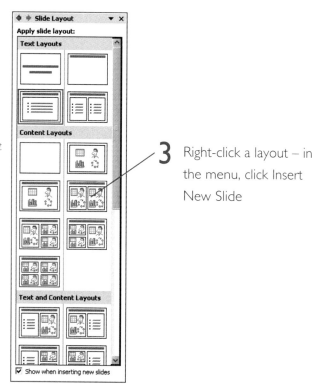

3 Right-click a layout – in the menu, click Insert New Slide

Inserting a slide from another presentation

1 In Normal or Notes Page views, move to the slide that you want to precede the new one

2 Pull down the Insert menu and click Slides from Files. Complete the dialog and click Insert

Inserting pictures

Inserting pictures via the Insert Clip Art Task Pane

In Normal or Notes Page views, go to the slide into which you want the clip art added. Pull down the Insert menu and click Picture, Clip Art. Now carry out the following steps:

1 Enter one or more keywords (these help you find clips)

3 Click Search

2 Optional – click here and make the appropriate choices

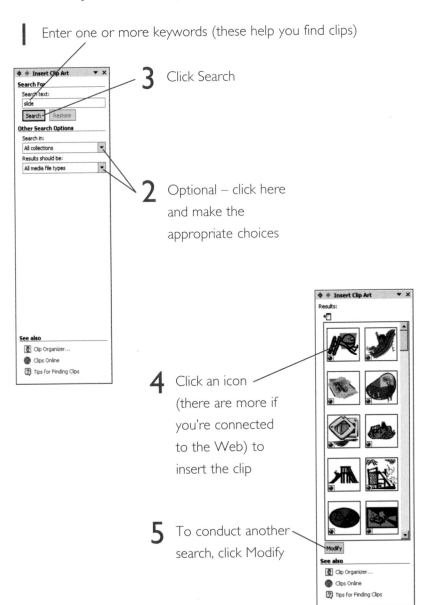

To add new clips to collections (or add new keywords to existing clips), click the Clip Organizer link at the base of the Task Pane.

4 Click an icon (there are more if you're connected to the Web) to insert the clip

5 To conduct another search, click Modify

...cont'd

Inserting pictures – the dialog route

In Normal or Notes Page views, go to the slide into which you want the picture added. Pull down the Insert menu and do the following:

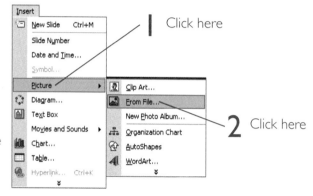

1 Click here

2 Click here

To have a picture appear on every slide, add it to the slide master (see pages 169–170).

4 Click here. In the drop-down list, click the drive/folder that hosts the picture

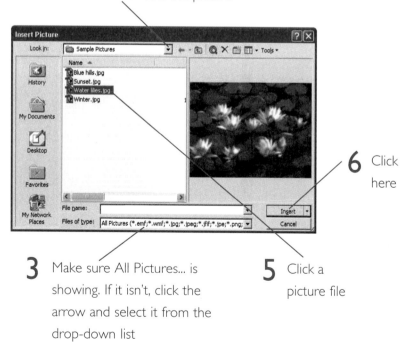

6 Click here

3 Make sure All Pictures... is showing. If it isn't, click the arrow and select it from the drop-down list

5 Click a picture file

Inserting diagrams

You can insert diagrams (e.g. pyramids and org charts) into slides.

I In Normal or Notes Page view, pull down the Insert menu and click Diagram

2 Click a diagram

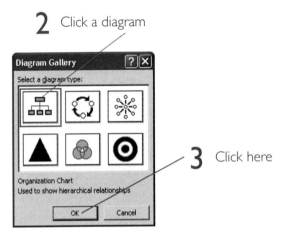

3 Click here

Use the Diagram toolbar to make any further changes e.g. click Change to to convert to another diagram or Layout to make layout changes.

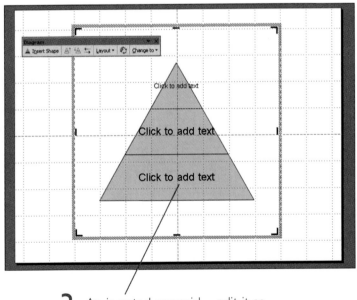

3 An inserted pyramid – edit it as required e.g. click a text placeholder and type in text, or resize it

Inserting animations

You can apply animations to slides. In PowerPoint, animations are defined as visual/sound effects applied to text and/or objects. You can apply standard animation schemes (often the best idea) or you can apply customized effects to specific objects.

Applying an animation scheme

1 Optional – in Slide Sorter view, select the slides you want to animate

2 Pull down the Slide Show menu and click Animation Schemes

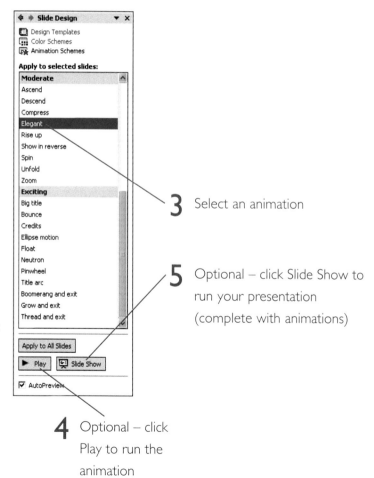

3 Select an animation

5 Optional – click Slide Show to run your presentation (complete with animations)

Click Apply to All Slides if you want the animation added to every slide.

4 Optional – click Play to run the animation

Customizing animations

1 Go to the relevant slide in Normal view and click the object you want to animate

2 Pull down the Slide Show menu and click Custom Animation

3 Click the Add Effect button. In the menu, select a category; in the submenu, select an effect

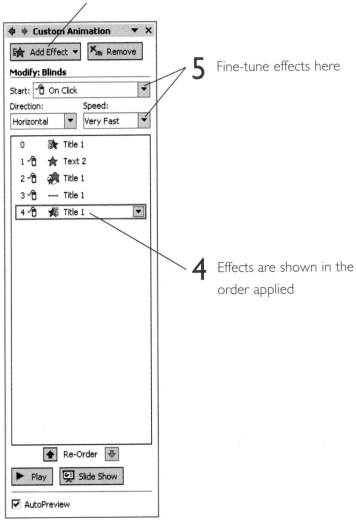

5 Fine-tune effects here

4 Effects are shown in the order applied

Inserting hyperlinks

You can insert hyperlinks into slides. In PowerPoint, hyperlinks are "action buttons" which you can click (while a presentation is being run) to jump to a destination. This can include a specific slide, a URL, another slide show or another file.

Inserting an action button

1 In Normal or Notes Page view, pull down the Slide Show menu and click Action Buttons. In the submenu, select a button

2 Position the mouse pointer at the location on the slide where you want the button inserted. Drag to define the button

3 Click here

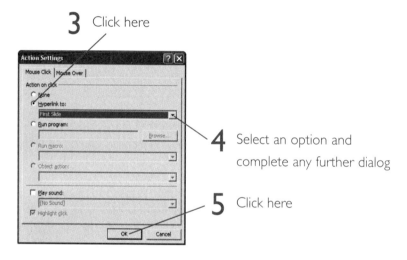

4 Select an option and complete any further dialog

5 Click here

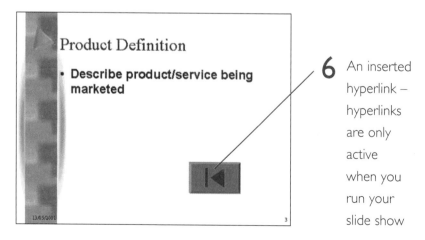

6 An inserted hyperlink – hyperlinks are only active when you run your slide show

Printing

You can print any presentation component. These include:

- slides

To preview a slide before printing, press Ctrl+F2.

- speaker notes

- outlines

PowerPoint 2002 makes printing easy.

Printing a presentation

Pull down the File menu and click Print. Now carry out any of steps 1–5 below, as appropriate. Finally, follow step 6.

1 Click here; select a printer

2 Click here to print the current slide only

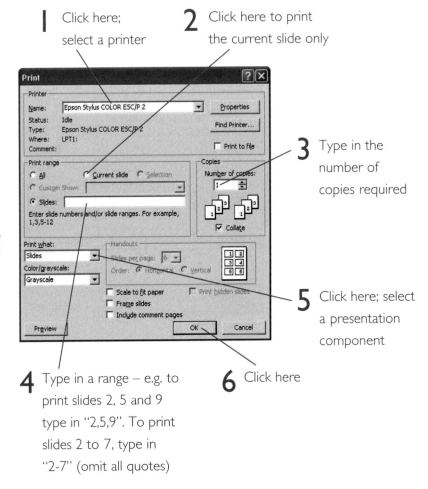

3 Type in the number of copies required

Ensure "Grayscale" and "Pure Black and White" are deselected in Color/grayscale if you have a color printer and want to print out in color.

5 Click here; select a presentation component

4 Type in a range – e.g. to print slides 2, 5 and 9 type in "2,5,9". To print slides 2 to 7, type in "2-7" (omit all quotes)

6 Click here

Running a presentation

Once you've created (and possibly printed) your slide show, it's time to run it. Before you do so, however, you should set the run parameters.

If you export slide shows to HTML format (see pages 183–184), you can view and run them in Internet Explorer.

When you run your presentation you can, if you want, have PowerPoint 2002 wait for your command before moving from slide to slide. This is useful if you anticipate being interrupted during the presentation. You retain full control over delivery.

Alternatively, you can have the slide show run automatically. Before you can do this, though, you have to set various parameters. These include the intervals between slides, which slides you want to run and the presentation type.

Preparing to run your slide show

First, open the presentation you want to run. Then pull down the Slide Show menu and click Set Up Show. Now do the following:

1 Select a slide show type (normally Presented by a speaker)

2 If you don't want all the slides to run, enter start and end slide numbers

3 Select a slide progression method (manual or at set times)

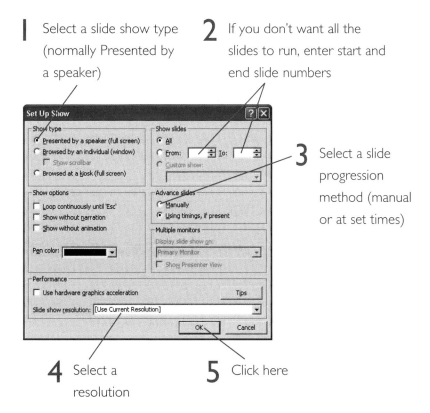

4 Select a resolution

5 Click here

Running a manual presentation

Pull down the Slide Show menu and click View Show. If you selected Manually in step 3 on page 181, PowerPoint runs the first slide of your presentation and pauses. When you're ready to move on to the next slide, left-click once or press Page Down. If you need to go back to the previous slide, simply press Page Up as often as required.

If you want to end your slide show at any time, simply press Esc. This applies to manual and automatic presentations.

Running an automatic presentation

Before you can run an automatic presentation, you have to set the slide intervals. You can do this by "rehearsing" the slide show.

Stage 1

Pull down the Slide Show menu and click Rehearse Timings, then do the following:

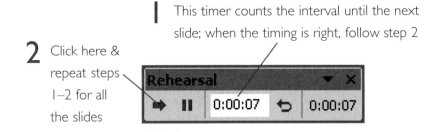

1 This timer counts the interval until the next slide; when the timing is right, follow step 2

2 Click here & repeat steps 1–2 for all the slides

After step 1, PowerPoint moves to the next slide. Repeat step 1 until all the slides have had appropriate intervals allocated. Finally, do the following:

You can also run your slide show on another computer (even one on which PowerPoint and Internet Explorer haven't been installed).

Pull down the File menu and click Pack and Go – this launches the Pack and Go Wizard. Follow the on-screen instructions.

3 Click here

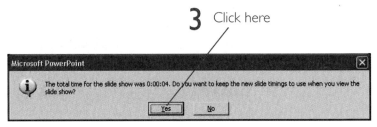

Stage 2

After rehearsal, pull down the Slide Show menu and click View Show. If you clicked "Using timings, if present" in step 3 on page 181, PowerPoint 2002 displays the first slide and moves on to subsequent slides after the rehearsed intervals have elapsed.

Running presentations in Explorer

One corollary of Microsoft's elevation of the HTML format to a status which rivals that of its own formats is that:

B. means that slide shows converted to HTML format and saved to the Web can be run by the majority of Internet users.

A.   presentations display authentically in Internet Explorer (especially if you're using version 4 or above)

B.   you can even run presentations from within Internet Explorer

Running slide shows in Internet Explorer

First, use the techniques discussed on page 17 ("Saving to shortcuts") to convert an existing presentation to HTML format. Open this in Internet Explorer. Now do the following:

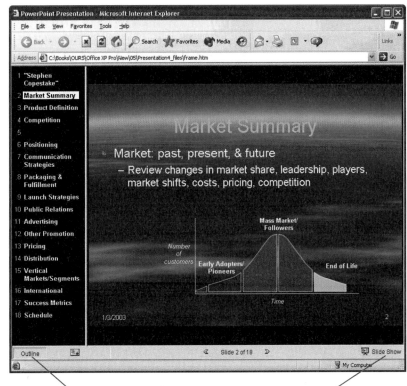

1   Click Outline to hide/unhide the slide outline

2   Click Slide Show to run your show in Full-Screen mode

Internet Explorer now launches the first slide of your presentation so that it occupies the whole screen:

To halt the slide show before the end, press Esc.

Whether or not you selected "Using timings, if present" in step 3 on page 181, Internet Explorer progresses to the next slide when the relevant interval has elapsed. And so on to the end...

3 When the last slide has been displayed, a special screen displays with the following text:

End of slide show, click to exit.

4 Click anywhere to return to Internet Explorer's main screen

Access 2002

Here, you'll become familiar with Access use. You'll create your own databases then go on to generate new tables and forms and move around through databases. Then you'll format your tables and forms, add new labels/fields and search for data. You'll create reports and convert data into charts. Finally, you'll customize database layout, preview your work and print it.

Covers

Chapter Six

The Access 2002 screen

Below is a detailed illustration of a typical Access 2002 screen:

This is Datasheet view, one of several ways of viewing and interacting with your data.

Menu bar Toolbar

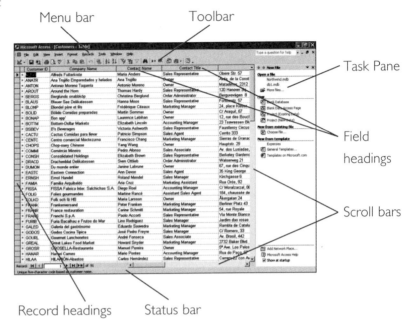

Task Pane

Field headings

Scroll bars

Record headings Status bar

Specifying whether the Status bar displays

Pull down the Tools menu and click Options. Then do the following:

Ensure the View tab is active

If you want to hide the Task Pane, uncheck Startup Task Pane.

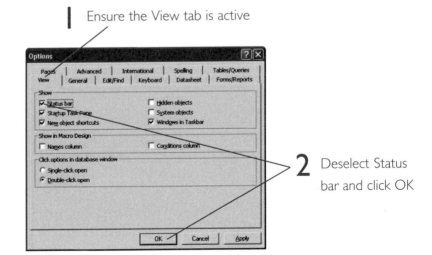

2 Deselect Status bar and click OK

Basic database terminology

Before you can learn to use Access 2002 to create databases, you need to be familiar with and understand the following terms:

Database   Information grouped together (and organized for ease of reference) into an Access file

Tables   Used to store data in rows/columns

Records   (Horizontal) rows of data in tables. Each record is a complete set of related data items.

Fields   (Vertical) columns of data in tables. Fields are spaces reserved for specified data

A further database component – reports – displays table data in a customized format (with page numbers and headings). Reports can't be edited, but they can contain data from one or more tables.

Fields

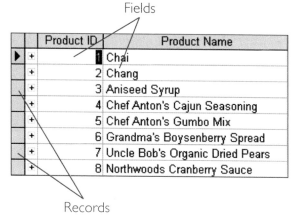

A table excerpt

Records

Tables, forms and reports are all "objects" and can be selected/ manipulated.

Forms   You use forms to display table data in a customized format. Forms display one record at a time, and are often the most convenient way to interact with your data. Below is a sample form:

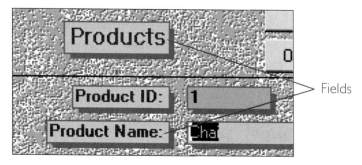

Fields

Automating database creation

Before you start to create a database, it's a good idea to plan it out first. Pre-planning can take various forms.

First, study how your data is currently organized and use this as a base. Second, be sure about the categories into which data can be split logically. Third, plan out which fields you need.

1 To create a database with the help of a Database Wizard, pull down the File menu and click New

2 In the Task Pane, click General Templates

3 Select the Databases tab

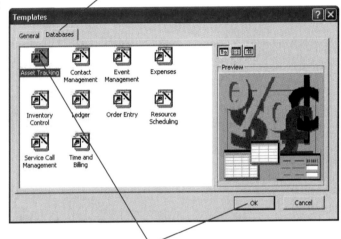

4 Select a template and confirm

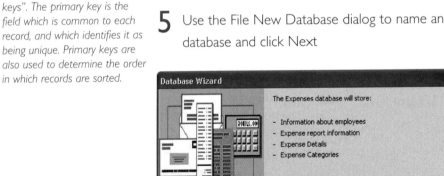

You should also determine which fields within specific tables can serve as "primary keys". The primary key is the field which is common to each record, and which identifies it as being unique. Primary keys are also used to determine the order in which records are sorted.

5 Use the File New Database dialog to name and save your database and click Next

6 Click Next

Repeat steps 7–8 as often as necessary.

7 Select a table for customization

8 Select and/or deselect fields

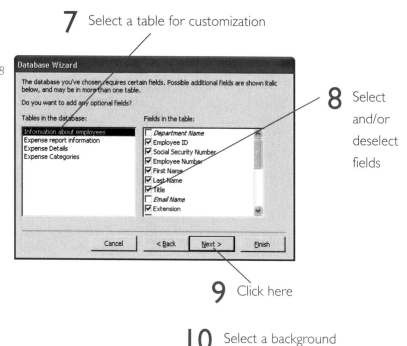

9 Click here

10 Select a background

11 Click here

12 Complete the remaining dialogs

The Database window

When you create a new database in Access 2002 (or open an existing one), the Database window displays. Since this is the basis for table creation, we need to discuss this before we move on.

| If the Database window isn't visible, press F11

Close button

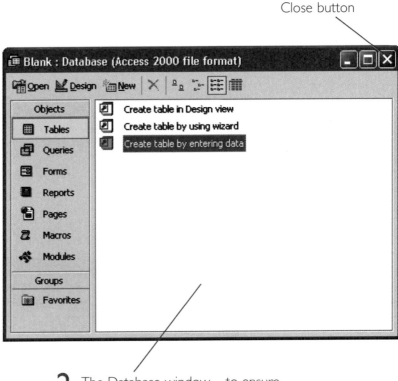

2 The Database window – to ensure that what the database window is displaying is up to date, press F5

The Database window can be thought of as a command center for the active database. For example, clicking on the Close button closes the database. It's also the basis from which much of the work you carry out with tables, forms and reports is undertaken.

Automating table creation

To create a table manually, select Create table by entering data in step 2 then amend the table design (see later).

1 Follow step 1 on the facing page

2 In the Database window, select the Tables tab on the left then double-click Create table by using wizard on the right

3 Choose a table category

5 Double-click the field(s) you want to include – they appear on the right

Data in tables is organized into columns ("fields") and rows ("records").

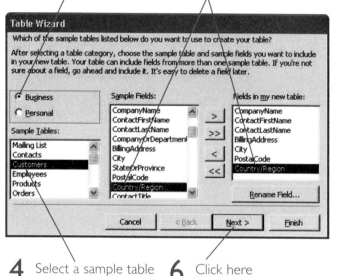

4 Select a sample table   **6** Click here

7 Type in a name for your table

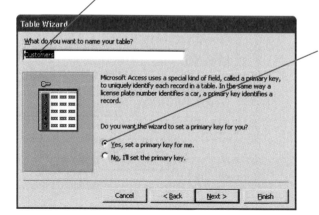

8 Opt to let Access set a primary key (often the best idea)

...cont'd

9 Select an option here – if you want to enter data straightaway, select either of the lower two options

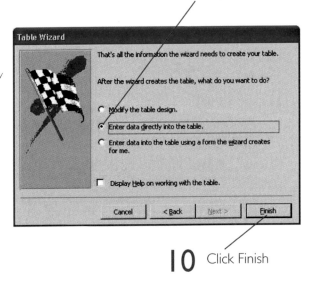

You can create tables from imported data. With the Database window active, choose File, Get External Data, Import. Double-click the Access file you want to import from. In the new dialog, select the Tables tab and double-click a table – Access adds it to the Database window.

10 Click Finish

11 If you selected Enter data into the table using a form... in step 9, start filling in the form

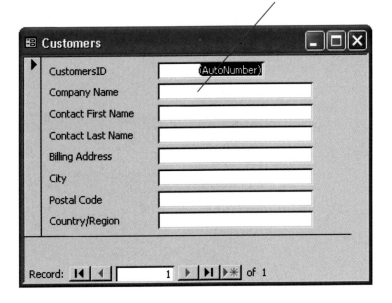

Amending table design

There are two ways to begin customizing a table's design.

If the table is already open
Pull down the View menu and do the following:

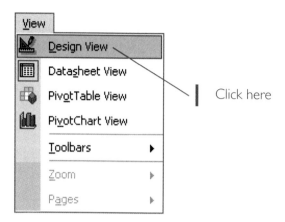

Click here

If the table isn't already open
Make sure that the Database window is visible. If it isn't currently on-screen, do the following:

1 If the Database window isn't visible, press F11

2 Select Tables on the left of the Database window

3 On the right of the Database window, right-click the table you want to amend

4 In the shortcut menu, select Design View

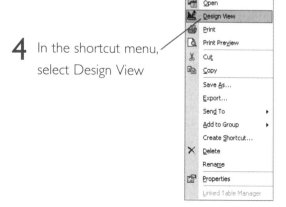

Design View window

The Design View window now launches. There are two sections:

When you close the Design View window, you're prompted to save your work.

Field Format pane

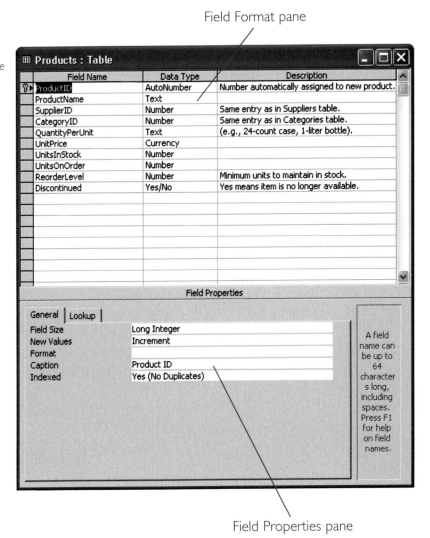

Field Properties pane

You can use the Design View window to set up new fields.

Setting up new fields

1 Follow the relevant procedure on page 193

3 Click here

Fields which have a key symbol set against them are primary keys.

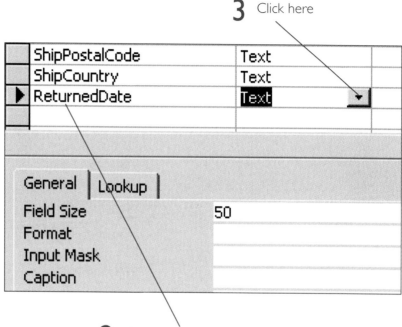

ShipPostalCode	Text
ShipCountry	Text
▶ ReturnedDate	Text ▼

General | Lookup

Field Size   50
Format
Input Mask
Caption

2 Click in the next empty field
and name the new field

All Access fields must have a data type. For more on data types, select one in the Design view window and press F1.

4 Select a data type –
AutoNumber (it enters
a unique ID reference
automatically) usually
needs no reformatting

Text
Memo
Number
Date/Time
Currency
AutoNumber
Yes/No
OLE Object
Hyperlink
Lookup Wizard...

Forms – an overview

Once you've created an Access 2002 database (and possibly one or more tables to go with it), you may well wish to create forms to view your data in a more "user-friendly" way. If you used a Database Wizard to create your database, you'll already have one or more tailor-made forms ready to use (even then, however, you may well want to create your own). If, on the other hand, you created the database manually, you'll have to create any forms you need. The procedures outlined here apply to both scenarios.

Using AutoForm

AutoForm produces simplified forms based on existing tables.

You can import forms from other Access databases. From the Database window, pull down the File menu and click Get External Data, Import. Locate the Access file then select the forms you want to import.

1 In the Database window, activate the Tables tab on the left then double-click a table

2 In the Table Datasheet toolbar, click the arrow next to:

3 In the menu, select AutoForm

4 The AutoForm appears – all fields and records in the base table display, and each field appears on a separate line:

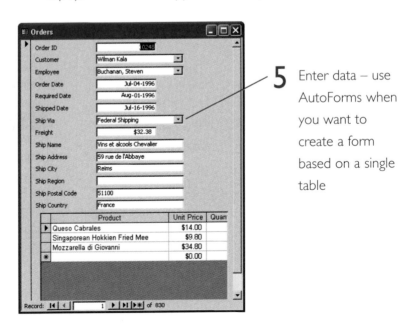

5 Enter data – use AutoForms when you want to create a form based on a single table

Automating form creation

To create a form with the help of the Form Wizard (i.e. when you want to create a form based on more than one table), first make sure that the Database window is visible. Do the following:

To open a form, double-click it in the Database window.

To create a form manually, carry out steps 1–2. Select Design View in step 3 then select a base table in the same dialog. Click OK. Access creates the new form in Design view (with easy access to fields in the selected table).

2 Click New

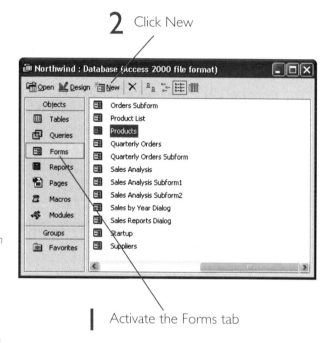

| Activate the Forms tab

3 Click Form Wizard

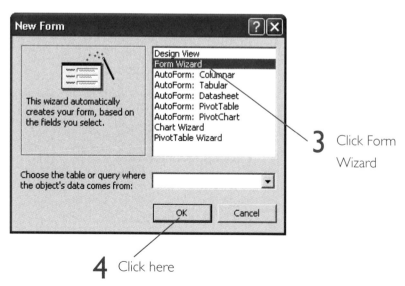

4 Click here

Access 2002 now launches the Form Wizard. Carry out the following steps:

If you want to use fields from additional tables, repeat steps 5–6.

5 Click here; select a base table in the list

6 Double-click the field(s) you want to include

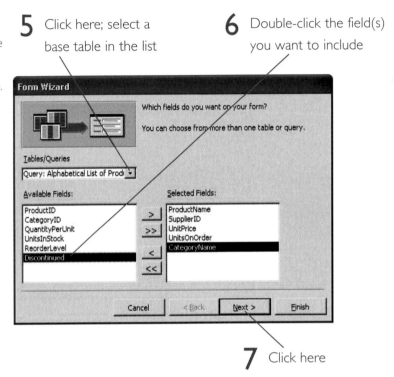

7 Click here

8 Click a form layout

9 Click here

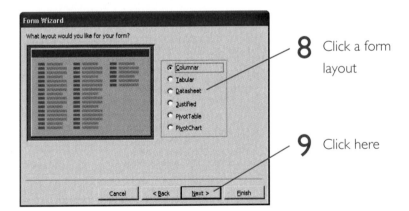

10 Complete the remaining wizard screens (select a style and name the form) then click Finish to create the form

Amending form design

There are two ways to begin customizing a form's design.

If the form is already open
Pull down the View menu and do the following:

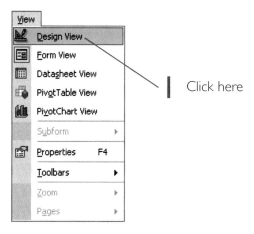

Click here

You can also use AutoFormat to apply a series of pre-defined formats to overall form design. With the relevant form open in Design View, press Ctrl+A. Choose Format, AutoFormat. Select a style and click OK.

If the form isn't already open
Go to the Database window and do the following:

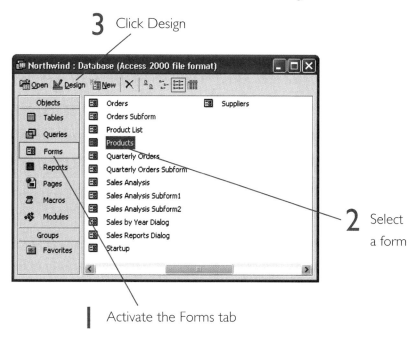

3 Click Design

2 Select a form

Activate the Forms tab

Customizing the form

Access 2002 now launches the form in Design View. This is the basis for adding and customizing fields. Design View's three principal components are shown below:

Detail pane   Field List

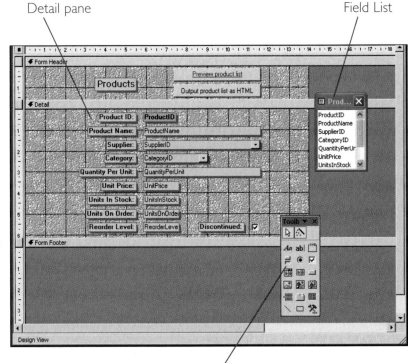

If the Field List or Toolbox aren't visible, pull down the View menu and click Field List or Toolbox respectively.

| Add more elements (e.g. check boxes) by dragging them from the Toolbox into the Detail pane

2 When you close the Design View window, you're prompted to save your work

The Detail pane

The Detail pane represents the current body of your form. Here, you create and design the necessary fields.

You can resize the Detail pane (or any other element) by dragging either of its edges (or the corner) outwards.

Adding labels

If the form header/footer area isn't currently visible, pull down the View menu and click Form Header/Footer.

It's useful to add descriptive labels to forms. You can add labels to the form header or footer and the Detail pane.

I   In the Design View window, refer to the Form toolbox and click this icon:

2   Move the pointer to the appropriate location in the header/footer or Detail pane. Drag to define the label area

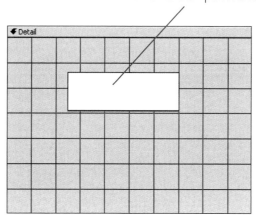

3   Type in the label text. When you've finished, press Enter

The end result:

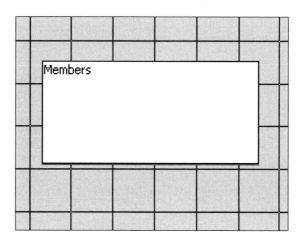

4   You'll need to reformat most labels after you've created them

Adding fields

Once you've inserted the necessary labels, the next stage is to insert the required fields. This is a simple process involving a drag-and-drop technique.

With the relevant form open in Design View, make sure the Field List is visible. (If it isn't, pull down the View menu and click Field List.) Then do the following:

Re step 1 – if no fields appear in the Field list, right-click the Detail pane. In the menu, select Properties. Click in the field at the top of the new dialog and select Form. Activate the Data tab then click in the Record Source field – in the list, select a base table.

1. Drag a field to the appropriate location in the form

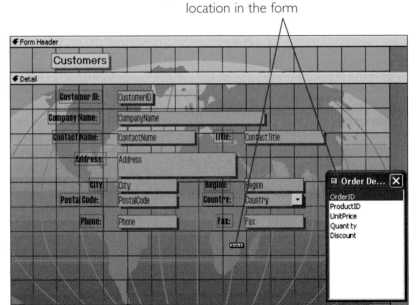

To add new fields to the Field List, open the table (in Datasheet view) which underlies the form. Click the column to the left of which you want the new column (field) inserted. Choose Insert, Column. When you reopen the original form, the new field appears in the Field List.

2. The new field is created – amend it as required

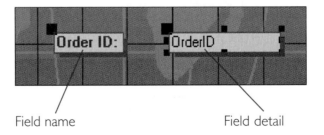

Field name   Field detail

Entering data

1 To create a new record in Datasheet or Form view, press Ctrl++

To insert the Euro symbol – € – into an Access 2002 field, hold down Alt and press "0128" (minus the quotes) on the numerical keypad to the right of your keyboard. Finally, release Alt.

+	WANDK	Die Wandernde Kuh	Rita Müller
+	WARTH	Wartian Herkku	Pirkko Koskitalo
+	WELLI	Wellington Importadora	Paula Parente
+	WHITC	White Clover Markets	Karl Jablonski
+	WILMK	Wilman Kala	Matti Karttunen
+	WOLZA	Wolski Zajazd	Zbyszek Piestrzeniewicz

A new record in Datasheet view

2 The new record

Customers

Customer ID:

Company Name:

Contact Name: Title:

Address:

City: Region:

Postal Code: Country:

Phone: Fax:

A new record in Form view

To cancel amendments you've made to the active field, press Esc.

3 Type in the necessary data and press Enter (the insertion point moves to the next field)

4 Repeat step 3 as necessary

5 If you don't want to enter data in a given field, press Enter or Tab (or Shift+Tab to reverse the direction) as often as necessary until the insertion point is in the correct field

6 When you jump to another record (see overleaf), Access automatically saves your amendments

Amending data

To edit existing database data, click the appropriate field in the relevant record (this applies to both Datasheet and Form views). One of two things happens now:

- if the field is empty, you can begin typing in data immediately

- if the field already contains data, Access highlights it. Simply begin typing and overwrite the existing data

Using the Zoom box

The Zoom box is, in effect, a special editing window which displays the whole of a field's contents, however extensive.

The next illustration shows the field detail section of an address field in a database form:

```
Brecon House
Fifth Floor
```

The address here consists of three lines, but only two display in the form. To view and/or edit the entire field, click in it. Then press Shift+F2. Now carry out the following steps:

| Type in replacement data, or click outside the highlighted text and make any necessary revisions

You can use the Zoom box in Form and Datasheet views.

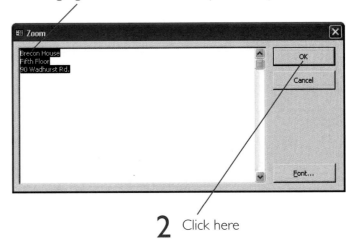

2 Click here

Database navigation

Using the Record Gauge

Press F5 to activate the Record Gauge. Then click as appropriate:

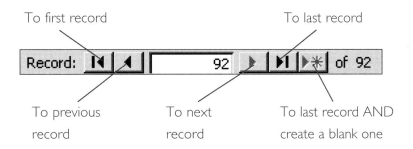

To first record

To last record

To previous record

To next record

To last record AND create a blank one

Using keyboard shortcuts

In Datasheet view, you can use the scroll bars to move to other records. In Form view, however, scroll bars move you to hidden areas of the current record.

The following keystroke combinations can be used to move around in both Datasheet and Form views:

End	Moves to the last field in the record
Home	Moves to the first field in the record
Ctrl+End	Moves to the last field in the last record
Ctrl+Home	Moves to the first field in the first record
↑	(In Datasheet view and tables only) goes to the active field in the previous record
↓	(In Datasheet view and tables only) goes to the active field in the next record
Ctrl+ ↑	Moves to the active field in the first record
Ctrl+ ↓	Moves to the active field in the last record
Page Up	Moves up by one screen
Page Down	Moves down by one screen
Ctrl+Page Up	(In Datasheet view) Moves one screen to the left
Ctrl+Page Down	(In Datasheet view) Moves one screen to the right

In Form view, Page Up and Page Down move to the previous or next record, respectively, when the start or end of the current record has been reached.

In Form view, Ctrl+Page Up takes you to the previous record, and Ctrl+Page Down to the next.

Spell-checking data

Spell-checking a form or table

1 Open a form or table

Access 2002 replaces some words/phrases automatically as you type (e.g. "mkae" becomes "make"). This is called AutoCorrect.

To add your own substitutions, pull down the Tools menu and click AutoCorrect. In the Replace field, insert the incorrect word; in the With field, type in the correct one. Click OK.

2 In the case of data in Datasheet view, select the record(s), column(s), field(s) or text you want to check. In the case of Form view, select the field or text you want to check

3 Pull down the Tools menu and do the following:

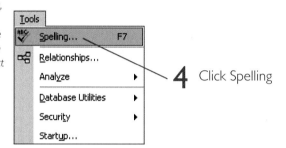

4 Click Spelling

5 If one of the suggestions here is correct, click it, then follow step 6

7 Click Ignore to ignore just this instance

8 Click Ignore All to ignore all future instances

6 Click Change to replace this instance

9 You have two further options. Click Add to have the flagged word stored in CUSTOM.DIC or click Change All to have Access substitute its suggestion for all future instances of the word

Saving to the Web – an overview

You can save database objects – in a variant of HTML or in XML format – to network, Web or FTP servers.

To import HTML or XML data, pull down the File menu and click Get External Data, Import. In the Import dialog, locate and select the relevant data file. Click OK. Complete the dialog(s).

HTML

When you export HTML files in Access 2002 they can be viewed directly from within Internet Explorer 5.x or later with little or no loss of data or formatting.

XML

You can also publish Access data on the Web in Extensible Markup Language (.XML) format, which specializes in describing/distributing data. Whereas HTML concentrates on describing how Web pages look, XML specifies how Web data is structured. How it's presented is the subject of a presentation file (called a "schema") which means that any application reading the XML data can present it in a host of different ways.

Another advantage of XML is that it's platform-independent: it can be utilized across the Internet, by different computers and applications.

Types of Web saving

Access 2002 lets you work with several different types of Web page. These include:

Dynamic HTML

Dynamic HTML files are also known as "server-generated" files and display as a table in any browser. To create a dynamic HTML file, output any table or form to ASP (Active Server Pages) format.

Use dynamic HTML for data which changes frequently and in any browser.

In order to save Web-format documents to network, Web or FTP servers, you need to have created a shortcut to the relevant folder. See page 17 for how to do this.

Static HTML

You can export any table, form or report to static HTML. In browsers, exported reports display as reports while tables and forms display in Datasheet view.

Use static HTML if you don't have access to the latest version of browsers or your data is not likely to be updated frequently and you don't want to interact with it.

Saving to static HTML

Exporting database components

1 In the Database window, activate the Tables or Forms tab on the left then double-click a table or form on the right

2 If you only want to export a portion of a table, pre-select it

3 Pull down the File menu and click Export

Re step 4 – carry out one of the following procedures according to your version of Windows:

- *Windows NT 4/98 users – use Network Neighborhood to save to a local network folder and Web Folders to save to a Web or FTP folder*
- *Windows 2000/Me/XP users – use My Network Places to save to a local network folder or to a Web or FTP folder*

4 Click here and select a recipient – see the tip

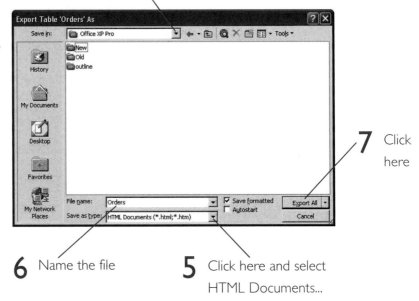

7 Click here

6 Name the file

5 Click here and select HTML Documents...

8 Ensure Save formatted is selected to save your HTML file in a format which resembles Datasheet view

9 If "Save formatted" was selected (see step 8) Access 2002 launches a special dialog. Click OK to create your HTML file with a default format

Saving to XML

Export your data to XML if you want to reopen it in Microsoft Excel.

1 Follow steps 1–4 on the facing page

2 In step 5 on the facing page, select XML Documents (.xml)

3 Follow steps 6–7 on the facing page

4 Specify what to export

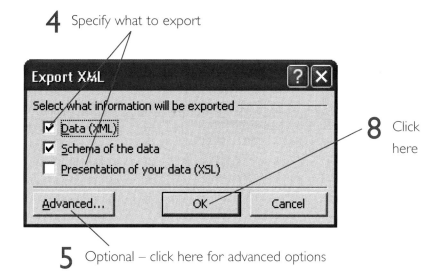

8 Click here

5 Optional – click here for advanced options

6 If you followed step 5, select a tab and make the relevant changes. For example, activate Data and specify where the file is saved. Or select Schema, choose whether to include a primary key and name the output file

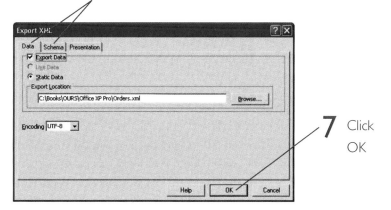

7 Click OK

Saving/publishing to dynamic HTML

You can't export reports to dynamic HTML.

1 Follow steps 1–4 on page 208

2 In step 5 on page 208, select Microsoft Active Server Pages (*.asp). You can also select Microsoft IIS 1-2 (*.htx; *.idc) – see your system administrator for more information

3 Perform steps 6–7 on page 208

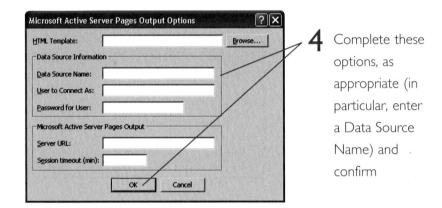

4 Complete these options, as appropriate (in particular, enter a Data Source Name) and confirm

5 On the computer which will process the dynamic HTML files, install the relevant software

The instructions here are guidelines to the overall procedure. Consult your system administrator for more specific information.

6 Create a folder to host the ASP files, then copy the files to it

7 Allocate the relevant privileges

8 Copy the appropriate database to the folder

9 Define the data source as a System DSN (Data Source Name) but make sure you use the name you entered in step 4

Find operations

Access 2002 lets you search the active database for text and/or numbers. You can:

- search through all fields within every record, or limit the search to a specific field in every record

- search forwards or backwards, or through the whole database

- limit the search to exact matches (i.e. Access 2002 will only flag data which has the same upper- and lowercase make-up). For instance, a case-specific search for "man" will not flag "Man" or "MAN"

To restrict the search to a specific field in every record, select the field before you launch the Edit menu then select it in step 2.

- limit the search to "match types" (the beginning of fields, the whole field or any part) – see step 4 below

Searching for data

Pull down the Edit menu and click Find. Carry out step 1 below, then steps 2–4, as appropriate. (Additionally, see the HOT TIPS for other ways to customize the search.) Finally, carry out step 5:

Re step 1 – you can also enter wildcards. "?" stands for any 1 character while "" stands for any number of characters (omit the quotes).*

To make searches case-specific, check Match Case.

1 Type in the data you want to find

2 Click here; select a field or datasheet/form to search

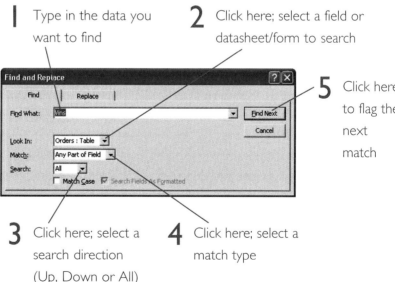

5 Click here to flag the next match

3 Click here; select a search direction (Up, Down or All)

4 Click here; select a match type

Repeat step 4 as necessary to locate further instances of the data specified in step 1.

Find-and-replace operations

When you search for data you can also – if you want – have Access 2002 replace it with something else. You can:

- search through all fields within every record, or limit the search to a specific field in every record

- search forwards or backwards, or through the whole database

- limit the search to exact matches (i.e. Access 2002 will only flag data which has the same upper- and lowercase make-up)

Replacing data

Pull down the Edit menu and click Replace. Perform steps 1–2, then 3–4 if relevant. Now do one of the following:

- Follow step 5. When Access 2002 locates the first search target, carry out step 6 to have it replaced. Repeat as often as required

- Carry out step 7 to have *every* target replaced automatically

If you want to restrict the search to a specific field in every record, select the field before you launch the Edit menu. Then select it in step 3.

If you need to make searches case-specific, check Match Case.

To specify a search direction, click in the Search field and select Up, Down or All.

1 Type in the data you want to find

2 Type in replacement data

5 Click here to flag the 1st occurrence

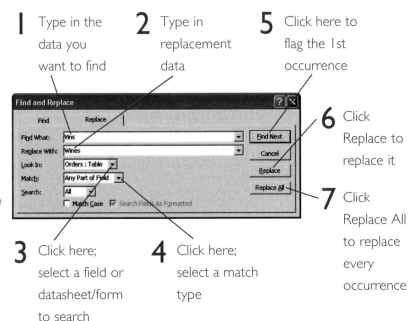

6 Click Replace to replace it

7 Click Replace All to replace every occurrence

3 Click here; select a field or datasheet/form to search

4 Click here; select a match type

Sorting data

Find operations locate records based on one criterion. However, you can also arrange records in a specific order; this is "sorting". Sorting helps you find data more quickly in tables and forms. You can sort data in ascending order (with this level of priority: 0 to 9 then A to Z) or in descending order (9 to 0, Z to A).

Carrying out a sort

In forms and tables in Datasheet view, you can sort by more than one field (from the left, but only in the same sort order). Simply select more than one column before you sort.

1 In either Datasheet or Form view, click the field on which you want to base the sort

2 Pull down the Records menu and click Sort, Sort Ascending or Sort, Sort Descending

Alfreds Futterkisten	Maria Anders
Ana Trujillo Emparedados y helados	Ana Trujillo
Antonio Moreno Taquería	Antonio Moreno
Around the Horn	Thomas Hardy
Berglunds snabbköp	Christina Berglund
Blauer See Delikatessen	Hanna Moos
Blondel père et fils	Frédérique Citeaux
Bólido Comidas preparadas	Martín Sommer
Bon app'	Laurence Lebihan
Bottom-Dollar Markets	Elizabeth Lincoln
B's Beverages	Victoria Ashworth
Cactus Comidas para llevar	Patricio Simpson
Centro comercial Moctezuma	Francisco Chang

Before the sort...

Centro comercial Moctezuma	Francisco Chang
Cactus Comidas para llevar	Patricio Simpson
B's Beverages	Victoria Ashworth
Bottom-Dollar Markets	Elizabeth Lincoln
Bon app'	Laurence Lebihan
Bólido Comidas preparadas	Martín Sommer
Blondel père et fils	Frédérique Citeaux
Blauer See Delikatessen	Hanna Moos
Berglunds snabbköp	Christina Berglund
Around the Horn	Thomas Hardy
Antonio Moreno Taquería	Antonio Moreno
Ana Trujillo Emparedados y helados	Ana Trujillo
Alfreds Futterkisten	Maria Anders

...after a descending sort has been applied to the field on the far left

3 To return your data to the way it was before a sort, choose Records, Remove Filter/Sort

Filtering data

Sorting data is one way of customizing the way it displays on screen. Another method you can use is "filtering". When you apply a filter, Access 2002 temporarily hides records which don't match the requirements ("criteria") you set.

Filtering involves:

- selecting the fields through which Access 2002 should search

- specifying the sort order (one particular advantage to filtering is that you can apply differing sort orders to the various fields)

- specifying what the fields must contain ("criteria") to have their records display

- applying the filter

Setting up a filter

In Datasheet or Form view, pull down the Records menu and click Filter, Advanced Filter/Sort – the Advanced Filter/Sort dialog launches. Do the following:

Repeat steps 1–3 for as many fields as you want to include in the filter.

Criteria are usually simple to use. For instance, you can use standard wildcards. "F" pulls in all entries beginning with "F".*

1 Double-click a field to have it appear in the Field box

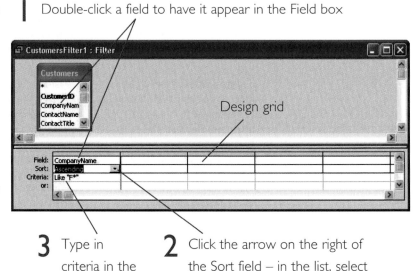

Design grid

3 Type in criteria in the Criteria field

2 Click the arrow on the right of the Sort field – in the list, select Ascending or Descending

When you filter data, the effects are only temporary: the underlying table is unaffected.

This method produces complex filters. Two simpler methods are Filter by Selection (you select a value and Access returns matching records) and Filter by Form (a version of the datasheet or form appears and you complete the relevant empty fields to match these).

Select these from the Records, Filter menu.

Applying a filter

Once you've set up a filter, the next stage is to implement it.

1 With the Advanced Filter/Sort dialog active, pull down the Filter menu and do the following:

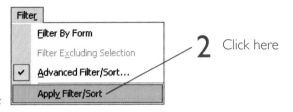

2 Click here

Removing a filter

When you've finished with a filter, you can deactivate it.

1 With the form or datasheet active, pull down the Records menu and do the following:

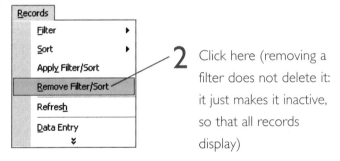

2 Click here (removing a filter does not delete it: it just makes it inactive, so that all records display)

Deleting a filter

When you've finished with a filter, you can erase it.

1 Click in the form or datasheet in which you created the filter

2 In the Records menu, select Filter, Advanced Filter/Sort

3 In the Edit menu, select Clear Grid, then follow steps 1–2 under "Applying a filter"

Reports – an overview

Forms allow you to enter data in a user-friendly way. Reports have a similar effect on the way you view (and print) data. When you create and view a report, however, you have:

To open a report, follow step 1 on the facing page then double-click its entry in the Database window.

- more control over the layout

- the ability to customize the printed output

Reports display data in a printed format but don't have to contain all the fields in the base table.

Preparation

Before you set up and institute a report, you should do the following:

1. examine your database, taking account of the current tables and forms

2. be clear in your own mind which components of your database represent data, and make sure you've entered all the data you want reports to display

3. if you want to enter data as well as view it, use a form (you can't enter information into reports)

4. if you've created previous reports (or if you've used a wizard to create a database and reports have been created automatically in the process, as is normally the case), review them with a view to highlighting areas which need improving

Report creation

You can create reports in three ways:

- with AutoReports (use these when you want to create a report based on a single table. With AutoReports, all the underlying fields display)

- with the Report Wizard (use this route when you want to create a report based on more than one table)

- manually

Creating AutoReport reports

To create a report manually, choose Design View in step 3. The report opens in Design view – add the necessary labels and fields.

Manually generated reports have to be saved – in Design view, choose File, Save As.

First, make sure the Database window is visible. Now carry out the following steps:

2 Click New

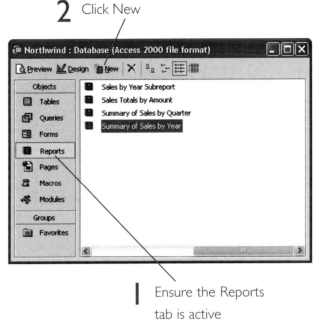

Ensure the Reports tab is active

In reports created with AutoReport, all fields/records in the base table display and each field appears on a separate line.

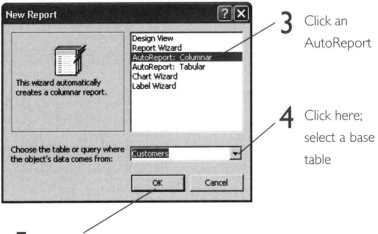

3 Click an AutoReport

4 Click here; select a base table

5 Click here – Access creates a report using the last AutoFormat you applied (see the tip on page 199) or the Standard AutoFormat

Using the Report Wizard

1 Follow steps 1–4 on page 217 (in 3, however, click Report Wizard) then click OK

2 Double-click the field(s) you want to include

Re step 2 – if you want to use fields from an additional table, click the arrow to the right of the Tables/Queries box. Make one or more selections from the list. Finally, double-click the relevant fields and carry out steps 3–5, as appropriate.

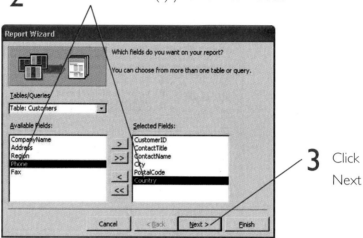

3 Click Next

4 Double-click a heading field (if any of the fields can be grouped under a convenient heading)

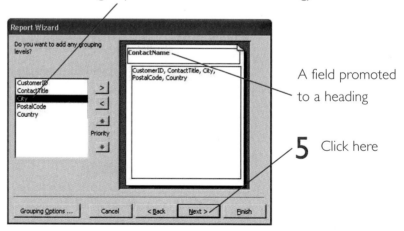

A field promoted to a heading

5 Click here

6 Complete the remaining wizard dialogs (select fields to sort the report by, apply a layout and style and name the report) then click Finish

Creating a graph

First, ensure the Database window is visible. Then carry out the following steps:

Viewing your data visually as a graph can make it easier to take in and absorb.

1 Follow steps 1–4 on page 217 (in 3, however, click Chart Wizard) then click OK

2 Double-click fields you want to include

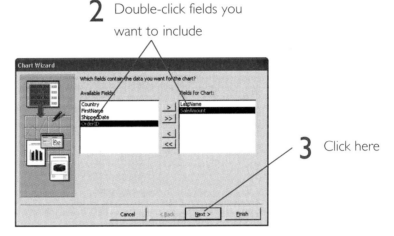

3 Click here

4 Select a chart type

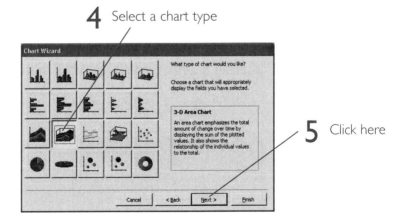

5 Click here

6 Complete the remaining wizard dialogs (select where you want the fields to go and name the chart) then click Finish to generate the graph

Page Setup issues

Page setup settings are stored with forms and reports, so you only have to enter them once for each component. With a table, however, you have to input them each time you want to print it.

1 In the Database window, activate the Tables, Forms or Reports tab on the left then double-click a table/form/report on the right

2 Pull down the File menu and click Page Setup. Do the following as appropriate:

Setting margin sizes

1 Ensure the Margins tab is active

In tables, ensure Print Headings is ticked to print column headings. (In forms, the field becomes Print Data Only. Check it to ignore gridlines, labels and borders when printing.)

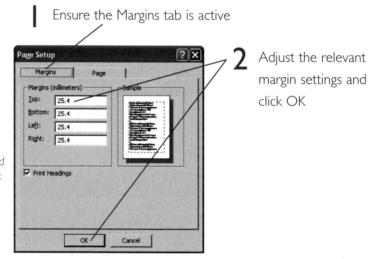

2 Adjust the relevant margin settings and click OK

Setting page size/orientation

1 Ensure the Page tab is active

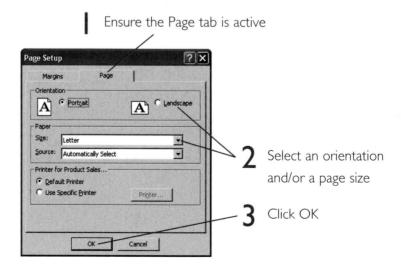

2 Select an orientation and/or a page size

3 Click OK

...cont'd

Specifying column layouts

In forms or reports, you can determine:

If you intend to print tables, forms or reports, you need to ensure that the correct page setup/layout settings are applied.

- how many columns data prints in

- the inter-column spacing

- the column width and/or height

- the gap between rows

- the order in which Access 2002 prints fields within records

1 In the Database window, activate the Forms or Reports tab on the left, then double-click a form or report on the right

2 Pull down the File menu and click Page Setup then do the following as appropriate

4 Type in the no. of columns   3 Activate the Columns tab

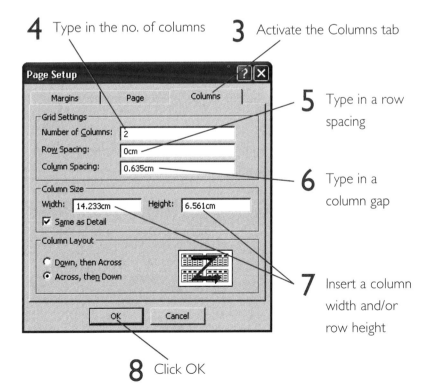

5 Type in a row spacing

6 Type in a column gap

Specify print direction in the Column Layout section.

7 Insert a column width and/or row height

8 Click OK

Using Print Preview

1 To preview a database component, choose File, Print Preview

2 Access 2002 launches a special Print Preview window showing how the component will look when printed:

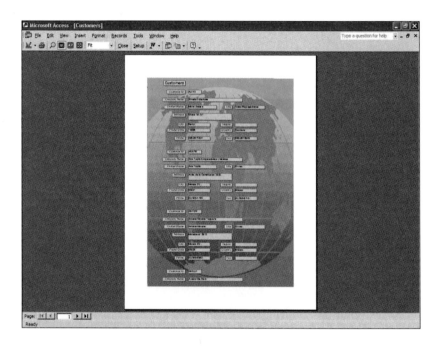

Using the Print Preview toolbar

1 Select any of the following in the toolbar at the top of the Print Preview screen:

No. of pages shown

Launch Help

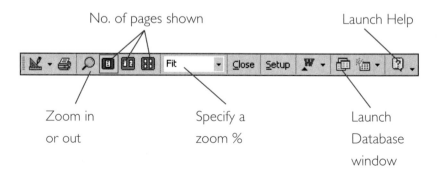

Zoom in
or out

Specify a
zoom %

Launch
Database
window

Printing your data

Stage 1 – preparing to print

First, preview the database component you want to print. Close the Print Preview window and launch the Database window. Then do the following:

You can print out your work with the current settings applying. This is a useful shortcut for proofing purposes. Just click this icon in the Standard toolbar:

1 Activate the Tables, Forms or Reports tabs, as appropriate

2 Double-click a table, form or report

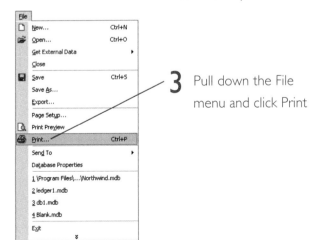

3 Pull down the File menu and click Print

If you print from within a form which is open in Design view, it prints in Form view.

Stage 2 – specifying the print settings

You can:

- specify the printer you want to use

- print the whole database component (the default)

- print a specific page range (e.g. pages 10–15)

- confine the print run to records you selected earlier

- specify the number of copies printed

- turn collation off or on. Collation is the process whereby Access 2002 prints one full copy at a time. For instance, if you're printing 5 copies of a 12-page database, when collation is active Access 2002 prints pages 1–12 of the first copy, 1–12 of the second copy, and so on...

Carry out any of steps 1–5 below. Finally, follow step 6:

1 Click here; select a printer in the list

If you need to adjust your printer settings, click Properties.

Print [?][X]

Printer
Name: Epson Stylus COLOR ESC/P 2   Properties
Status: Ready
Type: Epson Stylus COLOR ESC/P 2
Where: LPT1:
Comment: □ Print to File

Print Range
○ All
● Pages From: [ ] To: [ ]
○ Selected Record(s)

Copies
Number of Copies: [1]
☑ Collate

Setup...   OK   Cancel

2 Type in the number of copies

3 Uncheck this to turn off collation

5 Select this to print pre-selected records only

4 Type in start and end page numbers

6 Click here to start printing

Mail merging

Office's various modules are optimized to work together – in fact, that's precisely what makes Office XP Professional so useful. You can create a letter, format it, insert the appropriate fields and then "merge" it with a distribution list (for example, an Access database or your Outlook contacts) to produce a highly tailored result which you can then print and/or edit.

If all this sounds complicated, don't worry: Word's Mail Merge Wizard makes the whole process easy. You can even use the Wizard to produce mass emailings.

Covers

Chapter Seven

Mail merging – an overview

One of the strengths of the various Office XP Professional modules is that they work together very well, and the main way they do this is when you create and run a mail merge.

Mail merging is the process of:

You can also carry out a mail merge from within Access (when you do, Access hooks up with the Word Mail Merge Wizard).

In the Database window, select a table, form or report. Choose Tools, Office Links, Merge It with Microsoft Word and follow the instructions.

1. creating a "main document" in Word 2002 – this contains the text and/or pictures used in every copy of the final merged document

2. creating or opening a data source – this contains the information which is absorbed selectively into the main document. Data sources are basically lists of names and addresses

3. adding merge fields to the main document – these are placeholders. For example, you might have a field called "surname" which pulls in this information from the data source

4. merging data from the data source into the main document – this creates a new, merged document which is then printed (usually) or edited

Mail merging can be a fairly complex procedure. Luckily, you can use Word's Mail Merge Wizard (based in a special application of the Task Pane) to make it much easier and straightforward.

You can also use mail merging to:

*   create labels

*   create envelopes

*   create directories

*   create mass email

Mail merging between Word and Access or Excel is a great timesaver.

Running a mail merge

1 From within a new blank document in Word, pull down the Tools menu and do the following:

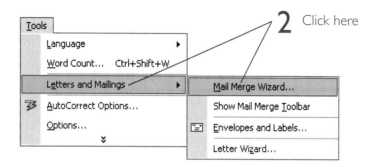

2 Click here

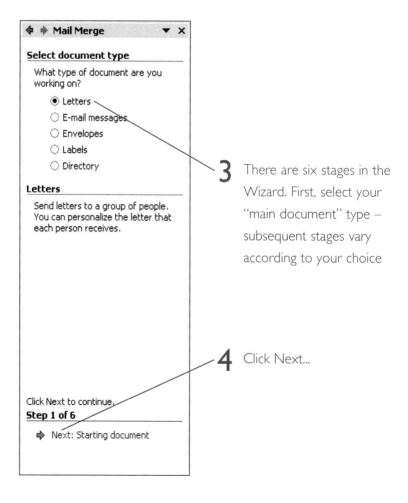

3 There are six stages in the Wizard. First, select your "main document" type – subsequent stages vary according to your choice

4 Click Next...

...cont'd

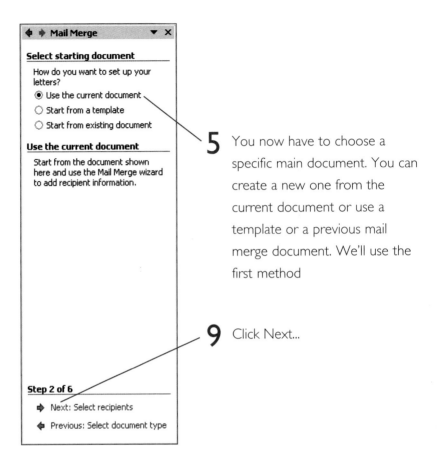

5 You now have to choose a specific main document. You can create a new one from the current document or use a template or a previous mail merge document. We'll use the first method

9 Click Next...

6 If you opted to use a template in step 5, a new link appears. Click Select Template and locate one in the dialog

7 If you opted to use an existing mail merge document in step 5, a new dialog appears:

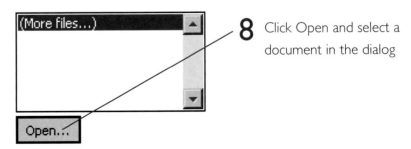

8 Click Open and select a document in the dialog

...cont'd

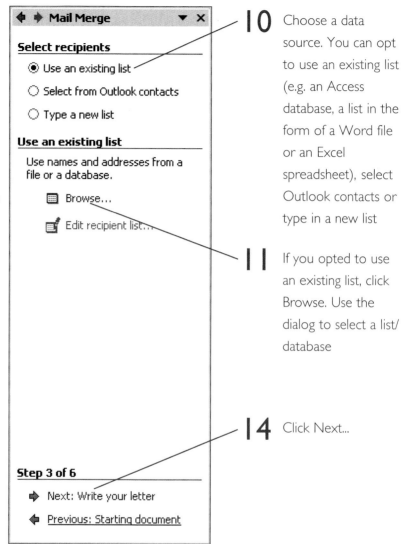

After step 11, two further dialogs appear if (as in this example) you opted to use an Access database as your data source. Select a table in the first. In the second, select/deselect recipients.

10 Choose a data source. You can opt to use an existing list (e.g. an Access database, a list in the form of a Word file or an Excel spreadsheet), select Outlook contacts or type in a new list

11 If you opted to use an existing list, click Browse. Use the dialog to select a list/database

14 Click Next...

12 If you opted to use Outlook contacts in step 10, click Choose Contacts Folder and follow the onscreen instructions

13 If you opted to create a new list in step 10, click Create... Access launches a form where you can enter contact information

15 It's now time to insert the necessary fields. Click in the appropriate location in your document then select a field type

To format merged data, you have to format the underlying merge fields. In the main document, select the field (including the demarcation characters to each side). Press Ctrl+D and complete the dialog.

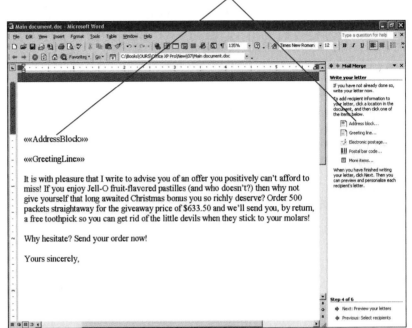

16 Complete the dialog which launches (this is an example) and click OK

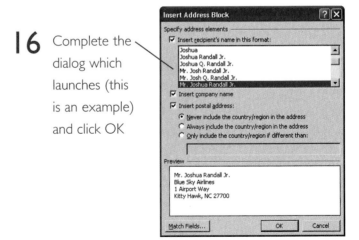

17 In the Task Pane, click Next: Preview your letters

18 Office merges your document with the selected data source and displays the first merged document:

Alfreds Futterkiste
Obere Str. 57
Berlin 12209
Germany

Dear Sir or Madam,

It is with pleasure that I write to advise you of an offer you positively can't afford to miss! If you enjoy Jell-O fruit-flavored pastilles (and who doesn't?) then why not give yourself that long awaited Christmas bonus you so richly deserve? Order 500 packets straightaway for the giveaway price of $633.50 and we'll send you, by return, a free toothpick so you can get rid of the little devils when they stick to your molars!

Why hesitate? Send your order now!

Yours,

Save your main document, so you can reuse it.

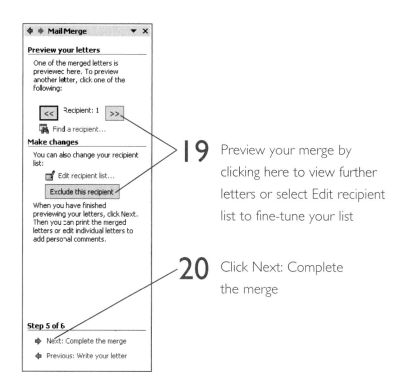

19 Preview your merge by clicking here to view further letters or select Edit recipient list to fine-tune your list

20 Click Next: Complete the merge

...cont'd

If, in step 3 on page 227, you selected an option other than Letters, this Task Pane may be different. For instance, if you selected E-mail messages, clicking Electronic Mail in step 21 produces a special dialog where you also specify To:, Subject line: and Mail format: options.

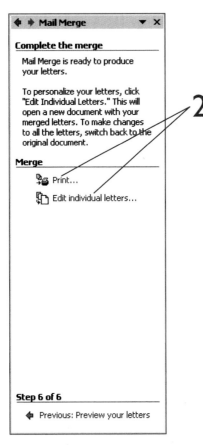

21 Merging is complete – you can send the merge results to your printer. Or you can send them to a new *superdocument* consisting of all the letters created by the merge – you can then edit this as required

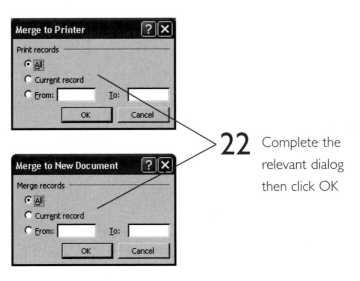

22 Complete the relevant dialog then click OK

Index

A

B

D

E